Project Team Dynamics

Enhancing Performance, Improving Results

D1502563

Project Team Dynamics

Enhancing Performance, Improving Results

Lisa DiTullio

ʃʃʃ
MANAGEMENTCONCEPTS

⟨⟨⟨ MANAGEMENTCONCEPTS

8230 Leesburg Pike, Suite 800
Vienna, VA 22182
(703) 790-9595
Fax: (703) 790-1371
www.managementconcepts.com

Printed in the United States of America

Library of Congress Cataloging-in-Publication Data

DiTullio, Lisa A.

   Project team dynamics : enhancing performance, improving results / Lisa DiTullio.
     p. cm.
   ISBN 978-1-56726-290-2
1. Teams in the workplace. 2. Performance technology. 3. Performance--
Psychological aspects. 4. Organizational effectiveness. I. Title.
HD66.D58 2010
658.4'022--dc22

                          2010026502

10   9   8   7   6   5   4   3   2   1

About the Author

Lisa DiTullio is the principal of Your Project Office, a PMI® Registered Education Provider and consulting practice dedicated to introducing project management as a business competency and enabling organizations to improve decision-making, instill accountability, and enhance communications. Her business offers training programs and advisory services that support project/business management and team-building activities, as well as virtual project office support services to organizations that do not need a full-time PMO.

Lisa is the editor of *ProjectBestPractices*, a quarterly newsletter from ProjectWorld, a regular contributor to the Silicon Valley PM and Project Connections blogs, and a contributor to *PM Network*. She is the author of *Simple Solutions: How "Enterprise Project Management" Supported Harvard Pilgrim Health Care's Journey from Near Collapse to #1*. She is a recognized international speaker in her field.

As past director of the PMO at Boston-based Harvard Pilgrim Health Care, Lisa was a core member of the turnaround team for an organization that went from being placed in state-supervised receivership in 1999 to being the "Number One Health Plan in America" in *US News & World Report* five years in a row.

Lisa is on the Board of Directors for the South Shore Chamber of Commerce and is past chair of the Women's Business Connection, a preeminent women's organization within the South Shore Chamber of Commerce. She is also a member of the ATHENAPowerLink® Governing Body, which oversees a program to provide women-owned businesses an opportunity to work with a panel of experts to grow their businesses.

Contents

Preface

In today's competitive environment, conducting business requires collaborative involvement across an organization. Project teams must include a number of participants from different areas of the organization. Parties from external agencies will also likely be involved, whether they are consultants or vendors. And in today's challenged economy, you are not guaranteed to get everyone you need, forcing you to make the most of your team and to do more with less. Regardless of who is on a project team and how many members it has, the project will not meet its deliverables and deadlines unless the group operates as a high-functioning team.

No matter what type of team you belong to, it's challenging to keep everyone focused and productive. This is particularly true on project teams. The secret to managing successful team dynamics is to keep the practices as simple as possible.

I love simplicity. Throughout my personal and professional life, I have always aimed for the least complicated path to find the answer or to complete the task. When communicating with others, I strive to impart my messages using short, tangible descriptions instead of long, abstract discussions. When teaching, I go out of my way to introduce concepts that are easy to grasp; they are often underscored through interactive activities so learners can experience the message rather than simply hear it. When speaking in front of large audiences, I design presentations that contain few words. White space and pictures help to spotlight my messages in a memorable way.

The simpler our business practices, the more likely we are to follow them. The more consistent we are with easy practices, the more likely we are to evolve corporate culture—ultimately embracing simple, effective, successful practices.

Enhancing team dynamics to improve team performance does not need to be complicated or time-consuming. In fact, the simpler you keep team-focused practices, the more likely you are to practice them consistently.

The extraordinary success of Apple suggests we are drawn to simplicity. From the hip design of its personal computers to the clever intuitiveness of its software to the sleekness of the iPod and the genius of the iPad, Apple consistently redefines each market it enters by creating gadgets with brilliant simplicity and ease of use.

Some people have a knack for making things more complicated than they need to be. I've found that to be the case, particularly when project managers make incorrect assumptions and become intertwined in an endless but futile effort to prove themselves right among team members.

When things get too complicated, change your assumptions and try again. Keep it simple to be successful.

This book will help you understand the value of teamwork and the link between teamwork and project/business outcomes: you will appreciate how simple investments in project team dynamics can provide big returns, you will learn how to introduce the "right" set of behaviors to support productive teamwork, and you will become familiar with easy methods to improve team dynamics and reduce conflict.

Some of the concepts and practices discussed in this book are derived from my experience managing the enterprise project management office (EPMO) at Boston-based Harvard Pilgrim Health Care. As a core member of the turnaround team for an organization that went from being placed in state-supervised receivership in 1999 to being named the "Number One Health Plan in America" by *US News & World Report* five years in a row, I have firsthand experience with the power of team-work and collaborative efforts.

Since leaving Harvard Pilgrim in early 2008 to establish my own training and consulting practice dedicated to introducing project management as a business competency, I have had the opportunity to work with many organizations across various industries that are looking to break down functional silos and deliver priority initiatives through effective and efficient means. This book is a compilation of best practices, tips, and techniques identified during my association with clients, colleagues, and project management professionals—all in support of healthy team dynamics.

You will find a number of tools and templates throughout the book, each designed to support a specific team need. An electronic version of each tool with a variety of templates, process tips, and techniques to support healthy teams is available for immediate download at the website *www.yourprojectoffice.com*. The tools and templates in this book and a variety of process tips and techniques to support healthy teams are available to download at www.yourprojectoffice.com. To access these resources, click on "Client Login" and enter username "Reader" and password "Team1." All the tools are formatted in MS Word or Excel, so no special software is required. If you have trouble accessing the site or its resources, please contact support@yourprojectoffice.com.

This book focuses on project teams. In the spirit of team achievement, many of the concepts, practices, and tools introduced in this book apply to all types of teams in business today. In fact, when you consistently apply similar practices across the different types of teams in your organization, you will slowly shift the organizational culture toward teamwork in a real and meaningful way. Organizations that appreciate the value of teamwork and perform in true team-like fashion tend to outperform those that only talk about teamwork. So feel free to share this book with other teams; they will thank you.

Introducing practical practices early in team development is critical to establishing healthy teams. Periodically evaluating the team's well-being is equally important; having the ability to quickly diagnose team ailments and apply appropriate treatments is key to hale and hearty teams, which result in productive and efficient output. This book supports both team launch and team operations; they are equally important to sustaining productive team output.

Those of us who are familiar with managing projects know that the greatest cause of project failure is lack of sound project planning. Benchmarks tell us projects fail when there is poor planning or estimating, no clear assignment of authority or responsibility, and a lack of adequate tools and techniques. Conversely, projects succeed when there is a high degree of end-user involvement, realistic expectations are set, ownership (both responsibility and authority) is apparent, and a clear vision and objectives are shared by all.

When launching project teams, a similar philosophy applies. Unless you establish a firm foundation, with qualified members who understand their roles and responsibilities and are vested in the team's success, the team will fail. Project team dynamics are just as critical to project success as proper project planning. Part I of this book focuses on launching a team. It guides you through a four-step process to properly establish a strong team foundation during early team formation—defining the team, clarifying team goals, implementing supporting behaviors, and establishing accountability.

In many organizations, project managers find themselves working with familiar faces with each new project assignment. Unfortunately, the comfort of familiarity often influences project managers to skip key team-building steps. The false sense of security aligned with the notion of "we've done okay before" often comes back to haunt such teams; teams that skip or skim over these steps frequently find themselves struggling later in the project. Remember, every project is unique; therefore, every team requires and deserves its own set of defined team goals, documented expected behaviors, and endorsed set of operating norms. The first part of this book, Launching the Team, will guide project teams through all four launching steps, offering practical advice and actionable steps for immediate results.

Once up and running, all teams inevitably face challenges that can cause tensions among members. Part II, Making the Team Work, addresses common ailments experienced by most project teams and offers straightforward techniques to address such disorders. Easy-to-use techniques, tools, and templates are included, offering you immediate opportunities to address and eradicate team afflictions. Four common aspects of poor team dynamics are addressed: managing team conflict, making effective decisions, actively sharing information, and holding productive meetings.

Because team dynamics are a key influence on project success, finding ways to better manage challenges from a management and communications perspective improves internal dynamics as well as group performance. Properly launching the team and quickly addressing team issues is a winning formula for enhancing performance and improving results.

Lisa DiTullio
Cohasset, Massachusetts

Introduction

It's always interesting to watch people who have been incredibly successful in their own businesses work in a group made up of equally strong personalities. It takes a special kind of leader who can effectively manage a team of veritable strangers and find the best way to get strong, winning performances from them.

—Donald Trump

Over the past decade, teamwork has received increased attention as more and more companies have recognized the power of cross-functional collaboration. Organizations are making every effort to bust functional silos and limit individual contributors. Business is too complicated to rely on singular heroes. Companies that embrace the power of collaboration realize that business problems are often solved when multiple people with different expertise and skills tackle the problems together.

Today, many business processes cut across departmental boundaries, warranting the involvement and input of many. In fact, company squads are everywhere—project teams, functional teams, cross-functional task forces, and steering committees. There seems to be a team for every type of business need.

TEAM REALITY

Have you ever watched the TV show *The Apprentice*? It is a reality show that originated in 2004 in the United States. Billed as "the ultimate job interview," the show consists of 16 contestants from around the country, each vying for an employment opportunity with Donald Trump. Businessmen and businesswomen compete in an elimination-style competition for a one-year, $250,000 job running one of Trump's companies. Each week the group is split into two teams, and each team is assigned a new "project manager." The project manager guides his or her team through project assignments. The team members endure long hours, grueling mental challenges, personality clashes, and intense scrutiny as they work together to complete assignments and beat the competition. The ninth season of the show will air in spring 2010; versions of the U.S. show can now be viewed in more than 20 countries.

To satisfy the voyeur in us, we tune in each week to experience the shaky, often volatile dynamics among contestants. Although the show focuses on the high drama among team members to emphasize the entertainment value, the scenes are not far from reality.

Whether you are a fan of the show or not, the weekly episodes depict the chaotic, highly charged realities facing teams in business today. And whether you like "The Donald" or not, he's right—teamwork is tough.

GROUP OR TEAM?

Before we introduce ways to promote healthy team dynamics, it's important to understand the differences between teams and work groups. Is your group a real team, a work group, or something in between? How you approach the development of your team or group will differ depending on the nature of the group, the duration of the project, the project scope, and the targeted project outcomes.

Don't confuse a group with a team. All teams are groups, but not all groups in an organization are teams.

The difference between a team and a group is that members of a team are interdependent for overall performance. In other words, a team is created when members are committed to a common purpose or set of performance goals for which they hold themselves mutually accountable. A group, on the other hand, consists of individual contributors, each vying for individual outcomes.

Teamwork is essential in today's global arena, where individual perfection is not as desirable as a high level of collective performance. A group qualifies as a team only if its members focus on helping one another to accomplish organizational objectives.

In today's rapidly changing business environment, project teams have emerged as a requirement for business success. Projects range in size and magnitude, and team sizes vary. But regardless of how short or long the project or how small or large the team, all projects are completed through groups, which tend to be complex from a management and communications point of view.

If you can improve group dynamics, you can improve project performance. The stronger the group, the better the performance. Therefore, all project team leaders should consistently facilitate the evolution of project groups into project teams. To achieve project success, everyone on the team must help one another achieve the project goal.

After receiving a project assignment, many managers are quite adept at guiding the project through its life cycle. Regardless of methodology type, experienced project managers instinctively know how to initiate, plan, execute, and close projects. Launching the project team, however, is not quite as intuitive—especially when corporate culture dictates most work relationships.

HOW CORPORATE CULTURE DRIVES BEHAVIORS

Knowing the difference between a group and a team is important; understanding the influence of corporate culture is critical. People in every workplace talk about *corporate culture*, a mysterious phrase that characterizes the work environment but is difficult to define. As someone once put it, "Corporate culture is how everyone behaves when no one is looking." Yet, even when it cannot be described, you usually know when you have found an employee or team member who appears to fit into your corporate culture.

Corporate culture should not be confused with the corporate mission. Corporate culture is the total sum of the values, customs, traditions, and meanings that make a company unique. It can often be identified through the philosophy and leadership style of the CEO; in fact, this is a much better indicator of corporate culture than the stated mission of the company. Simply put, corporate culture is about the traditions, ideas, and social behavior of an organization.

Senior leaders drive corporate culture; often, they impose corporate values and standards of behavior that specifically reflect the objectives of the organization. In addition, there is an extant internal culture within the workforce. Work groups within an organization also have their behavioral quirks and interactions, which to some extent affect the whole system. Hence, project teams can establish their own team culture, although doing so is difficult if the team culture does not somehow align with the corporate culture.

Throughout their life cycle, organizations tend to follow common evolutionary paths in their culture type, resulting in both advantages and challenges to organizational success. Taking the time to identify your organization's cultural type will help you leverage your team dynamics.

Let's consider how human system types drive behavior across an organization. David Kantor is a systems psychologist and organizational consultant who has made significant contributions to organizational development theory and practice. The Kantor System Typology and Communicational Domains™ includes four systems types:

- Random
- Open

- Closed
- Synchronous.[1]

Each of these systems contains characteristics and behaviors that either promote or impede business results, and each organization typically has a natural inclination toward one system or another, based on the industry in which it operates and its leadership style. Let's take a closer look at each.

Random Culture

A random culture, according to Dr. Kantor, is one that can be described as "individualistic." It is an environment that supports responsiveness, creativity, and entrepreneurship. When behavior is extreme, however, the organization can become chaotic and reactionary and can lack real direction. Table I-1 shows how Dr. Kantor describes a random culture.

Starbucks, the world's largest coffee shop operator, comes to mind when I think of a random culture. It is an organization that has found success in innovation, rapid expansion, and commitment to social responsibility. Yet, it is also an organization currently struggling to remain on top. As Starbucks seeks to restore what President and CEO

TABLE I-1   Random Culture[2]

Enabled (functional)	Disabled (extreme)
• Entrepreneurial	• Chaotic
• Responsive	• Conflict-ridden
• Competitive	• Duplication of effort
• Flexible	• No mutual problem solving
• Respectful of individuals	• Crisis-oriented
• Innovative	• Hard to get closure
• High-energy	• Lack of direction

Howard Schultz calls the "distinctive Starbucks experience," many analysts believe that Schultz must determine how to contend with higher material prices and increasing competition from lower-priced fast food chains.

Starbucks first announced it would discontinue its warm breakfast sandwich products (originally planned for nationwide launch in 2008) in order to refocus the brand on coffee, but then the sandwiches were reformulated to deal with customer complaints and the product line was retained. The sandwich line has since been repriced to compete more successfully with fast food chains.

In March 2008, Schultz made several announcements to Starbucks shareholders. He introduced Starbucks' new state-of-the-art espresso systems and also announced that the company hoped to enter the energy drink market. In June 2009, the company announced that it would overhaul its menu and sell salads and baked goods without artificial ingredients. The move is intended to attract health- and cost-conscious consumers without affecting prices.

The company continues its roller coaster ride. It recently cut U.S. expansion plans amid growing economic uncertainty and has dropped more than 1,000 non-retail jobs as part of its bid to reenergize the brand and boost profits. Not long ago it introduced Via instant coffee, comparable to fresh-brewed coffee. Some suggest it is Starbucks' last real chance for survival.

In spite of the shifts in focus and business challenges, Schultz has talked about making sure growth and change do not dilute the company's culture and the common goal of the company's leadership to act like a small company.

Open Culture

An open culture, described as "collaborative," is known for its open and constant communication. It relies heavily on teamwork and is adept at problem-solving. Yet, those who peer in from the outside might also view this culture as "all talk, no action." Table I-2 shows what an open culture looks like.

TABLE I-2 Open Culture[3]

Enabled (functional)	Disabled (extreme)
• Inclusivity	• Can't make a decision
• Diversity	• Too many meetings
• Empowerment at all levels	• All talk, no action
• Trust	• Frustrated members
• Direct communication	• Only vocal few reach "consensus"
• Negotiated outcomes	• Lack of strong leadership

Bluewolf, Inc., is an on-demand enterprise consulting firm headquartered in New York. It provides business consulting, IT resourcing, and remote database administration. Since 2000, Bluewolf has been the world's fastest-growing provider of on-demand software services, helping companies leverage the power of cutting-edge software applications.[4]

The vacation policy at Bluewolf sounds like a manager's worst nightmare. Employees at the consulting firm are allowed to take as much time off as they want, whenever they want. Extended vacations, trips to the movies, or watching a child's afternoon soccer game are all allowed, no permission required.[5]

In exchange for that freedom, employees must meet strict standards for success. Salespeople are evaluated on deals closed; consultants, on billable hours; and other employees, by customer satisfaction measures. Called "results only," the policy allows workers to take unlimited vacation time as long as they are performing according to expectations and are reaching their goals.

Bluewolf believes the more power it gives its people, the more responsibility they will take.

Best Buy has also adopted similar policies nationwide. At Best Buy, corporate employees are granted unrestricted time off. Empowered to make time-off decisions without guilt, most Best Buy employees take less time than their peers who have defined vacation and sick time policies.[6]

Closed Culture

A Closed culture can be described as "structured." It has stability, instills high levels of accountability, and is procedure-heavy. It typically contains strong leadership, is hierarchical in nature, makes quick decisions, and has efficient work processes in place. In other words, it is highly structured and productive. However, a closed culture can also be viewed as dictatorial, autocratic, and authoritarian. Table I-3 shows how Dr. Kantor describes a closed culture.

When I think about a company with a closed culture, the National Aeronautics and Space Administration (NASA) quickly comes to mind. It operates with a high level of precision, maintains very specific

TABLE I-3   Closed Culture[7]

Enabled (functional)	Disabled (extreme)
• Clear chain of command	• Tyrannical leadership
• Strong leadership	• Disempowerment
• Quick decisions	• Secrecy
• Efficient work processes	• Fear
• Commitment to goals	• Resistant to change
• Predictable service	• Lack of innovation/creativity
• Specific performance metrics	• Rule-bound and bureaucratic

performance metrics, and has a clear chain of command in place. NASA's mission is to pioneer the future in space exploration, scientific discovery, and aeronautics research.

President Dwight D. Eisenhower established NASA in 1958, partially as a response to the Soviet Union's launch of the first artificial satellite the previous year. President John F. Kennedy focused NASA and the nation on sending astronauts to the moon by the end of the 1960s. On July 20, 1969, Neil Armstrong and Buzz Aldrin became the first of 12 men to walk on the moon, meeting Kennedy's challenge.

NASA continues its scientific research and exploration. Its fleet of satellites is designed to help us understand how our world is changing, and NASA aeronautics teams are focused on improved aircraft travel that is safer and cleaner.

I spoke at a NASA event in 2007 and got a firsthand view of how methodically NASA employees perform their work. Procedural requirements often dictate how they conduct business. When you consider what NASA does and the precise requirements of its work, a closed culture is probably "right" for it.

Synchronous Culture

A synchronous culture can be described as "aligned." It has strong values, high levels of harmony, and a strong sense of direction. Table I-4 shows how Dr. Kantor describes a synchronous culture.

Google comes to mind when I consider a synchronous culture. Larry Page and Sergey Brin started the company as a research project in 1996, when they were both PhD students at Stanford University in California. They hypothesized that a search engine that analyzed the relationships between websites would produce a better ranking of results than existing techniques, which ranked results according to the number of times the search term appeared on a page. Originally, the search engine

TABLE 1-4   Synchronous Culture[8]

Enabled (functional)	Disabled (extreme)
• Strong purpose and vision	• Cult-like
• Aligned values and beliefs	• Inbred
• Harmonious interactions	• Discounts individual differences
• Low maintenance	• Minimal communication
• Efficient and effortless teamwork	• Low tolerance for ambiguity
• Implicit and understood roles	• Early closure on problems

used the Stanford University website with the domain *google.stanford. edu*. The domain *google.com* was registered in 1997, and the company was incorporated as Google, Inc., in 1998 in a friend's garage in Menlo Park, California.

The name "Google" originated from a common misspelling of the word *googol*, which refers to 10^{100}—the number represented by a 1 followed by 100 zeros. Having found its way into everyday language, the verb *google* was added to the *Merriam-Webster Collegiate Dictionary* and the *Oxford English Dictionary* in 2006. It means "to use the Google search engine to obtain information on the Internet."

Google has been known for its informal corporate culture, of which its playful variations on its own corporate logo are an indicator. Google's corporate philosophy embodies such casual principles as "You can make money without doing evil," "You can be serious without a suit," and "Work should be challenging and the challenge should be fun."

According to Sunil Chandra, Director, Human Resources, Technology and Operations at Google, staff are required, not just encouraged, to bring their laptops, Blackberries, and other electronic devices to staff meetings.[9] This supports Google's desire to enhance creativity at all times.

STRIKING A BALANCE

There is no "right" culture, but every organization has a tendency toward one of the four systems described above (see figure I-1). Dr. Kantor suggests that balanced systems are the most agile and are most likely to maintain success when facing adversity or the need to change. He also believes that cultural tension is most prevalent between

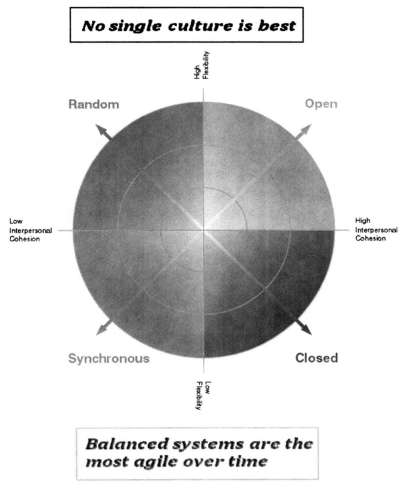

Figure I-1 Balanced Systems[10]

open and closed cultures. In fact, organizations that try to move from one to the other too quickly will certainly encounter significant challenges.

This is an important point because many organizations experience cultural change at some point in time. The catalyst driving cultural change might be from one of a variety of factors. A change in corporate leadership and the merger of organizations are the most common drivers for cultural change. Organizations with strong and adaptive cultures foster effective succession in the leadership ranks. In large part, the culture both prepares successors and eases transition.

When organizations want or need to change their culture, they can do so in a number of ways. The first is to lead by example. Leadership is critical in codifying and maintaining organizational purpose, values, and vision. Leaders must set the example by living the elements of the culture—the values, behaviors, measures, and actions. Values are meaningless without the other elements.

Culture must be made real through actions and team learning; it is much more than slogans and empty promises. At Baptist Health Care, for example, managers constantly reinforce the culture by recognizing those whose actions exemplify the organization's values, behaviors, and standards. Baptist Health Care rewards individual accomplishments through such things as "WOW (Workers becoming Owners and Winners) Super Service" certificates; appreciation cards for 90-day employees, which list their contributions to their team; one-year appreciation awards; and recognition of workers as "Champions" or "Legends" for their extraordinary achievements or service. Managers at all levels offer frequent informal recognition and send handwritten notes (which stand out in the age of email). Those who aren't living up to Baptist Health Care's values soon get the point.[11]

We need to bust functional silos in a lasting way. On project teams, this means we must embrace participant involvement and contribution, and at the same time eliminate functional identities that stymie team performance. This suggests that project team leaders must maintain a sensitive balance among team members. Subject matter experts are recruited to the project team for a reason, but their functional knowledge must blend with that of the other experts on the team for the project to be successful.

People must be open to learning new cultural norms and recognize that learning new behaviors does not require them to become someone they are not, but to improve on who they are. Just as each of us has probably gone through some type of exercise to increase our awareness of who we are and how we naturally behave, we should also take time to reflect on the culture in which we operate.

Complete the following sentences when assessing corporate culture:

1. My preferred system type is _____
   because _____

2. The system I have the most difficulty with is _____
   because _____

3. The system type I want to belong to is _____
   because _____

Every organization has a unique cultural identity and operates in its own way. This reality should always be considered when launching a team, particularly when you are combining a group of diverse individuals who come from different organizations (combining internal and external resources). We'll explore how to launch a team in part I.

Notes

1 David Kantor, *Inside the Family: Toward a Theory of Family Process* (San Francisco: Jossey-Bass, 1975).
2 Adapted from Kantor with permission.
3 Ibid.
4 For more information about Bluewolf, visit the company's website at http:// www.bluewolf.com (accessed June 8, 2010).

5 Information about the Bluewolf vacation policy is available at http://www.bluewolf.com/company/careers (accessed June 8, 2010).

6 Results Only Work Environment (ROWE) is a human resource management strategy co-created by Jody Thompson and Cali Ressler and originally piloted at Best Buy, where employees are paid for results rather than the number of hours worked.

7 Adapted from Kantor with permission.

8 Ibid.

9 Chandra spoke of Google's culture during his keynote address at the ProjectWorld Annual Conference in November 2008.

10 Adapted from Kantor with permission.

11 Al Stubblefield, *The Baptist Health Care Journey to Excellence, Creating a Culture that WOW's!* (Hoboken, NJ: John Wiley & Sons, Inc., 2005).

PART I

LAUNCHING THE TEAM

Project teams can become more efficient and effective by following four steps upon project assignment: define, clarify, implement, and establish. The chapters in part I focus on these four key steps:

Chapter 1. Defining the Team.   As the project kicks off, project team members are identified and recruited. Skill set, subject matter expertise, functional knowledge, and specialized experience must guide the resource selection process. A candidate's ability to perform in a team setting should also be assessed.

Chapter 2. Clarifying Team Goals.   As the group determines the project scope, sets the budget, plans the deliverables, and establishes the schedule, it is the perfect time to state team goals and define roles and responsibilities for each member of the group, as well as for the unit as a whole.

Chapter 3. Implementing Supporting Behaviors.   It's important to identify the specific actions and behavioral characteristics that will best support team goals and establish a team environment. Establish operating practices that allow everyone to be equally committed to a common purpose, set of goals, and working approach. In other words, everyone must agree to the team behaviors; they should not be set and imposed by the team leader.

Chapter 4. Establishing Accountability.   Discuss and decide how you and your team will be held accountable for meeting team expectations. Ideally, accountability is both individual and shared; effectiveness is measured by the group's collective outcomes and performance.

Many project teams naturally navigate the first two steps because most project managers have learned these practices during project management training. Many teams, however, skim or skip steps three and four, most often because of time constraints. Many project managers and team members find themselves hurled into the eye of the storm the minute a new project is assigned; with looming deadlines and high stakeholder expectations, less time is available for establishing team behaviors or setting team member accountability. Unfortunately, project managers often regret omitting these important steps.

CHAPTER I

Defining the Team

You put together the best team that you can with the players you've got, and replace those who aren't good enough.

—Robert Crandall

Studies suggest teams that perform well have a clear purpose, maintain open communication, and appreciate style diversity. Effective teams also rely on consensus decisions and have the ability to engage in civilized disagreements. On the other hand, team failure can result from a lack of trust among team members, vague assignments, and overbearing authority in a competitive, authoritarian environment.

The Blue Angels, established in 1946, are the epitome of a high-performing team. The mission of the Blue Angels is to enhance Navy and Marine Corps recruiting efforts by acting as positive role models and goodwill ambassadors for these military branches. They accomplish this through air performances; skilled pilots wow crowds with awe-inspiring air shows.

A Blue Angels' flight demonstration exhibits choreographed aerobatic maneuvers that use high-speed, low-altitude performance. Shows usually consist of a four-plane Diamond Formation, in concert with fast-paced, high-performance maneuvers of solo pilots. The show climaxes with the pinnacle of precision flying, performing maneuvers locked in as a unit in the renowned six-jet Delta Formation.

Safety is paramount for every demonstration. Each pilot must complete 120 training flights during winter training to perform a public demonstration. The teamwork required for high-speed, low-altitude flying in tight Blue Angel formation takes hundreds of hours to develop. All maneuvers are both mentally and physically demanding, and they reflect the challenges met daily by fleet Navy and Marine Corps aviators.

Each pilot is responsible for good health and safety; if the Flight Leader/Commanding Officer is grounded for medical reasons, the demonstration is canceled. This is one team that does not rely on backups or stand-ins. The teamwork required for formation flying takes many hours to develop, and a substitute pilot would not have enough time in the formation to perform safely.

Teamwork is vital for the Blue Angels. Without team collaboration, clearly defined roles, and constant communication, tragic missteps can occur. The Blue Angels conduct a Lessons Learned exercise at the end of every performance. They dissect their performance in exhaustive detail for an inordinate amount of time, always seeking opportunities for improvement. Blue Angel pilots capitalize on synergy, strive for perfection, and accept responsibility; they are a team prepared to win.

Although project teams in business today might not face the dire consequences the Blue Angels face when mistakes are made, there is good reason to aspire toward Blue Angel-like team performance. Such performance begins with defining the team.

GETTING STARTED

Congratulations! You've just received your new project assignment! As project manager, you are propelled into the project. You need human resources to help scope, plan, and execute the project on schedule and within budget. You need a variety of skills and expertise to support the project's complicated needs—and you need them quickly.

Sound familiar? Many project managers immediately find themselves thinking about *who* they need versus *what* they need when identifying project resources. In other words, many project managers select team members based on previous working relationships. Team members who hold required subject matter expertise and who performed well on previous projects are likely requested for future assignments; poor performers are seldom invited back.

This model works well when organizations have excess resources and support team culture. True team culture exists when members both demonstrate their best talents *and* function synergistically to achieve common goals. Unfortunately, many organizations lack both the bandwidth in resource availability and the true team mindset. As a result, project team leaders often find themselves fighting for the same small pool of ideal team members. There are never enough star players to fulfill all project team requirements, forcing project team managers to staff with "B" players.

Identifying what is needed on the team rather than who you want on the team is a great way to approach functional managers when requesting resources. When you are able to describe the skills, expertise, and assets of what you need on the team, you are effectively informing managers how to develop other staff members who might not quite have what it takes to make the team today. This has long-term value for both you as the requesting manager and the functional manager. Having large pools of highly qualified staff maintains the delicate balance between supporting project needs and meeting operational requirements without depleting the "A" players.

Be willing to accept rookie players. New members bring fresh perspective to solving project challenges, there's nothing like a fresh set of eyes to solve an old problem.

Aside from selecting team members who hold the "right" level of skill and expertise needed to support the project requirements, it is just as important to identify team members who are able to work well with others and exhibit consistent levels of cooperation. These "social intelligence" skills include the ability to persuade, negotiate, compromise, and make others feel important.

Team members come in all shapes and sizes, with varying levels of training, expertise, experience, education, and background. Some team members come with extensive industry and/or subject matter expertise, whereas others do not; many fall between the two extremes. The challenge you face as a project manager is to know what you want in a team member before you search for one. Be thoughtful and precise in assessing the level of skill you need (to support the size, type, and magnitude of your project), and overlay those requirements with emotional, social, and interpersonal intelligence requirements.

In fact, be careful not to overemphasize technical requirements when evaluating candidates. Limiting your search to people who have strong technical capabilities but lack professional decorum and interpersonal skills is not likely to produce optimum project results. Project members who have subject matter expertise but lack collaboration, tolerance, and understanding are not likely to fit well on the team; instead, they are more likely to alienate their teammates. Project team members who can get the job done but will leave a trail of destruction in their path are less-than-ideal candidates for any team.

Projects cannot afford team turnover. The challenge is this: How do you select the "right" team players?

SELECTING TEAM MEMBERS

Screening project team members requires project managers to see beyond accomplishments and credentials. The traditional screening questions still apply when assessing project team members. They typically include:

- Tell me about yourself.
- What are the roles and responsibilities of your current position?
- What size projects have you supported in the past?
- What is the average length of the projects you have been involved in?
- Have you participated in project teams on a full-time or a part-time basis?

Because many organizations today do not have enough resources to adequately support project teamwork and ongoing operations, many team members (as well as project managers) are asked to support project work during their "free time." They might also be expected to participate on multiple projects at once. With so much juggling going on, it is easy to bypass a thorough team selection process in order to launch the team quickly. It is easy to ask only the screening questions, which might not get you all the information you need.

Beware. Not taking adequate time to evaluate potential team members in advance of placing them on the team might cause regret later—for you as the team leader, for the individual team members, and for the team as a whole. To see past a candidate's resume or technical expertise, take the time to evaluate the person thoroughly. Using behavior-based methods to screen team candidates has become increasingly popular—and necessary.

The premise behind behavioral interviewing is that the most accurate predictor of future performance is past performance in similar situations. The key is delving deeply enough during the interview process to accurately assess past behavior. Behavioral interviewing requires that the interviewer ask questions in a way that reveals a candidate's true character. The interviewer must probe to reach a depth of detail that forces the candidate to share past team experiences and behaviors. Interviewers must ask pointed questions to elicit detailed responses that reveal whether the candidate possesses the ideal team characteristics.

Suppose, for example, you ask, "How would you handle XYZ situation?" The responder has minimal accountability. However, suppose you ask, "What were you thinking at that point?" or "Lead me through your reasoning for how you handled that situation." This tactic is apt to provide far more insight about the candidate and his or her ability to handle tough situations. Continuous probing of a specific situation puts the pressure on. It also enables you, as the interviewer, to observe the candidate's ability to hold up under a barrage of difficult questions.

When you create a line of questions designed to uncover a candidate's true personality, you can discover "multiple intelligences" to determine whether the candidate will meet the requirements of the position and fit into the team culture. The phrase *emotional intelligence* was coined by Yale psychologist Peter Salovey and University of New Hampshire psychologist John Mayer to describe qualities like understanding one's own feelings, empathy for the feelings of others, and "the regulation of emotion in a way that enhances living."[1]

In October 1995, *Time Magazine* published an article on emotional intelligence in which the authors suggest that a triumph of the reasoning brain over the impulsive one is emotional intelligence. Regardless of our cognitive ability (i.e., IQ), each of us has an emotional intelligence that natural talent seems to ignite in some people and dim in others.[2]

In the area of emotion, the distinction between intelligence and knowledge is murky and debate continues today around our own ability to distinguish between the two. There is, however, enough evidence to suggest that plenty of "smart" people have little understanding of their emotions and don't know how to use emotions in their communication and relationships. Conversely, many "feelers" have a natural tendency to dismiss logic and rational approaches. Neither type of person will fit well into any team unless he or she is able to find and maintain balance.

In addition to assessing a candidate's technical experience and emotional intelligence, it is also important to assess the candidate's work style and work/life balance philosophy. For example, it is beneficial to understand the candidate's position on putting in extra hours when a project require extra dedication, his or her preferred method of communication, and how he or she deals with stress as a project races toward the finish line or encounters significant risks. Understanding working characteristics allows you to fully evaluate the candidate and anticipate how he or she will fit into the group.

As you screen candidates, be sure to delve into their minds by asking questions about when they have been successful or what they would have done differently. Assess the candidate's ability to be a team player. Look for responses that suggest the candidate accepts accountability, takes psychological responsibility and pride, and talks about previous team relationships openly. Too much reference to "I" or not enough sense of accountability for the work efforts suggests the person might not really be a team player.

Team building starts in the interview process. When conducted properly, the process is designed to ferret out personalities that might not fit on your team. Always meet with the candidate more than once to get a true read. This is often difficult in the fast-paced business environment we operate in, but it is important nonetheless. Sometimes the connection is instantaneous, but always meet twice with a person to double-check your gut reaction and instinct.

It is also helpful to invite others to participate in the screening process. Include potential peers, other confirmed team members, project sponsors, or key clients who have good interviewing and people skills. Having a candidate meet with different interviewers helps validate your reaction or highlight something you might have missed.

For organizations that rely primarily on internal resources to fulfill project team requirements, do not assume that because you have worked with a potential team member on a previous project he or she will automatically meet the needs of the new project assignment. Every project is different; every potential team member should be considered on the basis of the requirements of the current project.

Consider the following questions, even if you have worked with the prospective team member in the past:

• Does this candidate have adequate experience and skills in participating on this type of project?

- Does this candidate have previous experience on similar-sized projects?

- Does this candidate have balanced control over his or her emotions? The ability to handle stress?

- Is this candidate ready for a bigger challenge?

- What level of self-awareness has this candidate reached in relationship management? Social awareness? Self-management?

- If I have worked with this person previously, what do I know about his or her technical abilities and social interaction skills that concerns me or confirms to me that he or she is the right fit for this new team?

Table 1-1 provides some example interview questions to help you select the "right" team members.

For most of the questions in table 1-1, you can continue to probe the candidate by delving deeper into the situation. Ask, "How did you feel at that time?" "What did you do next?" Ideally, each question posed will peel back an additional layer of the candidate's personality, allowing you to assess the fit on the team.

INFORMING TEAM CANDIDATES

As the team leader, you are responsible not only for selecting the "right" members for your team but also for informing potential team members what is expected of them once they join the team. Don't confuse this step with defining roles and responsibilities for confirmed team members; that comes later in the project launch and team-formation process.

This step is a precursor to defining team member roles and responsibilities. It enables you as the team leader to inform team candidates what you expect of all team members once they join the team and lets you view their reaction before you ask them to join the team.

TABLE 1-1   Behavioral Interview Questions

Describe a project or idea that was implemented primarily because of your efforts. What was your role? What was the outcome?

Describe a major change that occurred on a past project. How did you adapt to this change?

Give a specific example of a time when you used good judgment to solve a problem.

Tell me about a time when you had to analyze information and make a recommendation.

Give a specific example of a time when you had to deal with conflict on a team. What was the problem and what was the outcome?

Tell me about a time when you had to establish rapport quickly with someone under difficult conditions.

Some people consider themselves "big picture" people while others are "detail-oriented." Which are you and why?

Give me an example of when you were able to successfully communicate with another person during a particularly difficult time.

What challenges have occurred while you were coordinating work with other team members or projects?

Describe a time when you took ownership for conflict with another.

Give an example of when you had to reach a quick decision with limited information.

Tell me about a time when you had to defend a decision.

Describe a recent unpopular decision you made and what the result was.

Tell me about the most difficult person you have ever had to work with and how you managed to work with the person (or not).

Have you ever made a mistake because you did not listen well to what someone had to say?

Have you ever been dissatisfied with a team member's work? How did you handle it?

There are times when people need extra help. Can you give an example of when you were able to provide support to a teammate?

Give an example of an important goal that you set in the past. Did you reach it?

TABLE 1-1   Behavioral Interview Questions (*Continued*)

How many hours a day do you put into your work?
Give me an example of how you have influenced change.
What excites you?
Describe a time when you were asked to keep information confidential.
Tell me about a time when you had to handle a tough problem that raised challenging ethical issues.
Give me an example of a project that best describes your organizational skills.
How do you prepare for a presentation to a group?
How would you describe your presentation style?
Can you describe a time when you were less than pleased with your performance?
Please give an example of when you have worked cooperatively with others to accomplish an important team goal.
Describe the types of teams you have been involved with. What were your roles?
Describe a team experience you found disappointing.
Describe a time when you had to adapt to a culturally diverse environment.

For example, candidates for the Blue Angels are made aware that they will be away from home a lot before they volunteer for duty with the team, and the pilots are selected in part on the basis of their ability to cope with not only family separation but also a strenuous practice and show schedule.

Many project teams experience a turnover in team membership throughout the life of the project. This happens for a variety of reasons, including voluntary resignations, reductions in workforce, and changes that require additional or different resources to support new needs. Regardless of why team changes occur, be prepared. A change in team membership will affect the group, regardless of how high-performing the team might be.

When selecting new members to join an existing team, take care to ensure that new members will fit with existing team members. This is particularly important with project teams in full implementation mode; new team members must quickly adapt to existing team practices and also be able to contribute to the team in a seamless manner.

As team leader, you will have little time to fully assess how a new team member will fit into the existing team culture. When you interview the new candidate, include one or two other team members in the screening process. If possible, invite the potential new team member to meet with the existing team as a whole, so everyone can get a feel for one another. The best approach is through a face-to-face session; virtual teams will need to adjust their screening and assessment processes accordingly.

Forming a project team should be a deliberate act in which candidates are considered in terms of the skills and experience they offer and their motivation to participate and to contribute to the team as a whole. Ideally, team members should be equally committed to the project goal and to the health of the team, have a clear sense of roles and responsibilities, and be accountable for getting things done as and when needed.

Once you have selected your team members, you must begin to solidify the team. One way to do this is to clarify team goals. We'll explore ways to collectively clarify team goals in the next chapter.

Notes

1 Peter Salovey, Marc A. Brackett, and John D. Mayer, eds., *Emotional Intelligence Key Readings on the Mayer and Salovey Model* (Port Chester, NY: Dude Publishing, 2007).
2 Nancy Gibbs, Sharon Epperson, Lawrence Mondi, James L. Graff, Lisa Towle, "The EQ Factor," *Time Magazine*, October 2, 1995.

CHAPTER 2

Clarifying Team Goals

Teamwork is the ability to work together toward a common vision. It's the ability to direct individual accomplishments toward organizational objectives. It is the fuel that allows common people to attain uncommon results.

—Andrew Carnegie

Building a team is a combination of selecting individuals, assigning them to project roles within an overall project structure, and ensuring the team members share the same view of why they are together and what they are trying to achieve. Contrary to what you have practiced in the past or what you might have been told, clarifying team goals does not need to be a time-intensive step in the team-formation process.

Benchmark data show us time and time again that projects fail when there is poor communication, skills are mismatched, or there are resource shortages. Alternately, we know project success occurs when there is a high degree of end-user involvement, executive management actively supports a project, realistic expectations are set, and there is accountability.

Project success is further promoted through effective communications, efficient risk management, and a hard-working, focused project team. Efficient operational handoffs are also a key success element.

We know that teams perform well when they have a clear purpose, they have unmistakable roles and work assignments, and there is active participation and collaboration among team members. For project teams to succeed, a project manager must ensure that:

- *Team roles and responsibilities are clearly defined and communicated.* Ideally, only one person should be accountable for one or multiple things, although any number of team members may contribute toward a deliverable.
- *Roles are clarified, with clear lines of accountability and reporting relationships.* This is particularly true when staffing a large program that requires a large number of resources over a long period of time.
- *A clear project organizational chart is created once all team members are confirmed.* The chart must be updated if the project team changes.

Much of this work can be accomplished as the project progresses through the initiation and planning phases; the more information you have about the goals and objectives of the project, the easier it is to define team roles and responsibilities. Likewise, the team objective is normally tied to the project objective, but it might look at that objective from the team's perspective on quality, delivery schedules, and cost/incentive accomplishments.

PROJECT GOALS AND OBJECTIVES

Before we focus on team goals, let's take a minute or two to talk about project goals and objectives. It is critical that everyone understands the project's goals because this is one of the best ways to turn a group into a team. Having the project clearly defined is a great starting point to ensure everyone has the same shared vision and is working toward the same outcomes.

In other words, everyone on the project team should be able to answer the key question, "What are we doing?" Unless everyone is capable of answering this question with confidence, accuracy, and consistency, there is little chance that the group assigned to execute the project will do so successfully, let alone transition from a group to a team during the project's life cycle.

All project team members should be able to answer key questions as the project transitions from one phase to the next. Using a four-phase life cycle, here are the key questions to be answered for each phase:

- Initiation: What are we doing?
- Planning: How do we do it?
- Execution: Are we doing it?
- Close: Did we do it?

High-performing teams are able to answer each question with ease and familiarity. Each team member is actively involved in the project work, openly shares project information, and supports the other team members throughout the life of the project.

PROJECT INITIATION AND PLANNING

There are a number of ways to effectively guide the team through the project initiation and project planning processes, ensuring all project stakeholders have a shared understanding early in project launch and during team formation. Conducting project initiation and project planning workshops is an effective and efficient way of reaching team consensus on what the project is and why it is being launched.

Project Initiation Workshop

The Project Initiation Workshop (PIW) is a structured meeting designed to initiate a project. The benefits of such a workshop include creating a communication device whereby all key stakeholders agree on what the project will do and why they are doing it. The workshop includes the opportunity to obtain organizational expertise and experience to further define the project, and it establishes ownership to plan the project. The initiation process typically includes six steps.

1. *Draft the project scope.* Solidify the project's opportunity and goal with senior management and other key stakeholders. (A stakeholder is anyone who has an impact on or is affected by the project.)

2. *Complete PIW pre-meeting activities.* Establish workshop goals and attendees, formalize the workshop agenda and timing of topics, and establish roles.

3. *Prepare PIW.* Plot the major project scope sections, send meeting notice with applicable handouts, ensure key participant attendance, and prepare meeting room accordingly.

4. *Conduct PIW.* Establish the foundation of the project, obtain "buy-in" of the organization, and build the project planning team.

5. *Document PIW.* Finalize the project scope document and get sponsor signature, and document project planning team members.

6. *Communicate PIW results.* Communicate "the project" to all stakeholders.

To be successful, a PIW requires all the "right" participants. Attendees to consider include project stakeholders, functional managers (if they control the personnel resources you will need to plan or do the project), operational recipients (anyone who receives project deliverables in their operational environment as a result of the project), project sponsors (anyone who funds the project), and anyone who can help define and determine the boundaries of the project.

The number of right participants can lead to a lengthy invitation list. Try to keep the group small if you can; focus on the key decisionmakers from each participant category. The foundational group of invitees for the PIW must include decisionmakers for the workshop to be successful. Most project initiations occur quickly, leaving little time for adequate meeting preparation and planning. As with any meeting, it is important to have an agenda. Figure 2-1 is an example of an agenda designed to successfully guide the PIW session.

The example agenda includes generic agenda items to support a productive PIW. The agenda should be adjusted to meet individual project

<*Team or Project Name*>
Project Initiation Workshop Agenda
<*Logistics: Date, Time, Location, Call-In Numbers*>

Attendees:

Facilitator(s):

Overall Meeting Goal: Obtain stakeholder agreement on what the project will do & why it is being done.

Duration	Agenda Topic	Who	Goal
	Introductions, workshop purpose, review agenda and ground rules		
	Project risks, assumptions, issues & decisions will be simultaneously recorded		
	Review the business opportunity and project goal		
	Determine project scope		
	Determine project deliverables		
	Determine expected business outcomes by their success metrics		
	Validate that deliverables are aligned with the business outcomes and the project goal		
	Determine the high-level milestones		
	Complete the flexibility matrix		
	Determine (additional) planning team members		
	Determine "next steps"; assign owners and due dates to risks, assumptions and issues; schedule next meeting		
	Workshop evaluation		

Figure 2-1 Example of a Meeting Agenda

needs; feel free to revise the wording and timing of items, delete steps you do not require, or add steps not listed but relevant to your specific project. To help you determine which agenda items are most valuable for your project initiation activities, table 2-1 provides some additional details for each agenda item in figure 2-1.

Facilitating a successful PIW requires sound time-tracking. Realize the implications of staying on certain subjects, and manage the expectations as to what will or will not be accomplished as a result. The timing and duration of activities are highly variable, based on project size, number of stakeholders, deliverables, etc. Schedule enough time; it is better to let participants go early than to keep them late. In some instances, you may want to assign a timekeeper to ensure the group remains on track and on time; acting as both facilitator and timekeeper can often be difficult.

Finally, never skip the "next steps" agenda item. Skip something else if you have to.

The agenda is designed to guide participants through an exercise to identify and document key elements in support of defining the project's scope. All project teams must take the time to define the project and the project team. The Project Opportunity Statement (POS) is a terrific way to define and document the project scope.

Project Opportunity Statement

The POS is the foundational scope document that specifies the business opportunity, the project goals and deliverables, and the expected business outcomes the project will deliver to the organization. Ideally, the executive sponsor reviews and approves the project scope once it is drafted. (His or her signature represents the initiation of executive sponsorship accountability.) Once approved, it becomes the foundation for future planning and execution of the project. It also becomes the reference document for questions or resolving conflicts over the project's purpose and scope. The value of this tool is that it can sustain constant use, regardless of project size, type, or scope.

TABLE 2-1 Agenda Details

Agenda Topic	Typical Duration	Process/Expectations	Tip
Introductions, workshop purpose, review agenda and ground rules	10 minutes	• Introductions can be made round-robin • Review "boarded" meeting goal; use a pre-plotted agenda, visible to all • There are usually no issues with this process	• Start on time • Use a quick ice-breaker
Review business opportunity and project goal	30 minutes	• Read the plotted sections to the team • Take minimal feedback and edits (markup of the plot) to these sections	• Get executive sponsor to agree to these sections prior to session • Get sponsor to kickoff session • Do not rewrite!
Determine project scope	30 minutes	• Define what "scope" is and how it works • Review drafted entries on plotted sheets, discuss, take feedback, and edit plots directly	• Take this as an opportunity to introduce the project's method for managing change

(Continued)

TABLE 2-1   Agenda Details (*Continued*)

Agenda Topic	Typical Duration	Process/Expectations	Tip
Conduct stakeholder analysis	15 minutes	• Define a "stakeholder" • Prompt the team for entries • Create a list on an easel sheet	• Stakeholders stand to gain and lose • Don't miss any! They get deliverables!
Determine project deliverables, their completion criteria, and timing	45 minutes	• Define "deliverables" • Add/change/delete on deliverable section of plot • Collect qualifying criteria	• Use your stakeholder analysis to help determine whether you have all of your deliverables
Determine expected business outcomes, their metrics, and timing	20 minutes	• Review drafted entries on plotted sheets • Discuss and take feedback • Edit plots directly	• If you cannot define specifically, use ranges
Validate deliverables are aligned with business outcomes and project goal	10 minutes	• Read completed/plotted entries • Query group for cause/effect • Make adjustments/ edits as necessary	• Make sure you are aligned now!

Task	Time	Details
Determine high-level milestones	20 minutes	• Review drafted entries on plots • Discuss, take feedback • Make edits to plots directly • Build "sticky note" timeline, augment with new, get dates • Review "typical" milestones • Stay at a macro level
Complete the flexibility matrix	10 minutes	• Introduce and communicate "triple constraint" to group • Use a prepared easel sheet to communicate and dicuss • Get the project sponsor to define this prior to the meeting • Do not change it at the meeting
Determine the planning team members	10 minutes	• Explain the planning commitment • List required representatives and their roles • Get names, capture on easel • Get the names or dates • Name planning team • Publish it
Determine next steps	15 minutes	• Ensure all risks, assumptions, issues, and decisions are identified • Identify owners and due dates • Plan and schedule the PPW ahead of time and announce to group, if possible
Workshop evaluation	10 Minutes	• Ask team for suggestions/feedback on how meeting went • Capture and discuss • Don't get defensive • Just take feedback

The POS consists of 17 components, all critically important to defining project scope.

1. *Business Opportunity/Problem Statement.* The opportunity defines the particular business opportunity or problem being addressed by the project. It contains statements of well-known fact that everyone in the organization will accept as true.

2. *Project Goal.* A project has one overall goal which concisely summarizes what will be delivered by the project that addresses the business opportunity. The goal provides a continuous reference point for any questions regarding the purpose of the project. For example, "Design and implement XXX system."

3. *Constituents.* This component allows you to identify all constituents who are impacted by the project.

4. *Line of Business.* This component allows you to designate the line(s) of business impacted by the project.

5. *Project Scope.* The scope identifies which aspects of the business are to be included in the project and which are to be excluded. It determines what other external influences and impacts (such as interfaces, customer needs, and regulatory requirements) are to be addressed. It can range from business process scope and business product scope to organization scope, application scope, or "other."

6. *Expected Business Outcomes.* These are the criteria by which the *business* success of the initiative will be determined.

7. *Major Project Deliverables/Measuring Project Completion.* The deliverable statements define what constitutes *project* completion. They state what must be accomplished to achieve the business outcomes and reach the project goal. The major project deliverables should describe what is to be accomplished (i.e., a future state; typically a noun) and an action (i.e., how the deliverable will be delivered; typically an action verb). A planned date and measures of completion help to clarify deliverables.

8. *Major Milestones.* Use this section to document the milestones (events) that must occur in order to reach the deliverables noted in the section above.

9. *Applicable Life Cycle/Methodology.* This allows identification of any other life cycle/methodology that is required to support project requirements (i.e., product development life cycle).

10. *Committee approvals.* Project teams often need to obtain approvals from executive sponsors or steering committees. Such parties are identified here.

11. *Assumptions.* These are factors that, for planning purposes, will be considered true, real, or certain. They are important because many noted assumptions represent a risk.

12. *Risks to Project and Contingency Plans.* Risks are factors that might interfere with the project work. For example, internal risks are factors that the project team can control or influence, such as staff assignments and cost estimates. External risks are factors beyond the project team's control or influence, such as market shifts and government action. If any risks might be assumed, this section should include contingency plans for addressing them.

13. *Dependent Initiatives.* It is important that the project stakeholders understand how this project is linked to other work in the organization.

14. *Core Team Personnel Resources.* Document the skill sets and/or specific people this project will need for its core team. It is important to estimate the extent of commitment necessary for each personnel resource. (Detailed resource requirements for the entire project will be determined after the planning phase of the project is complete.)

15. *Alternatives Considered.* Note any other approaches that the team considered when preparing this project. Explain why those alternatives were rejected.

16. *Financial Analysis—Quantitative.* Define the financial impact of the project. If the project is being justified on the basis of financial return, a detailed cost/benefit analysis should be provided.

17. *Authorized to Proceed.* This is where the executive sponsor signs this document, approving the start of project activities.

The PIW is designed to address the following components of the POS:

- Business Opportunity/Problem Statement
- Project Goal
- Project Scope
- Expected Business Outcomes
- Major Project Deliverables
- Major Milestones.

Again, the POS template can be easily adjusted to meet your project and/or business needs. Feel free to ignore headings if they don't apply or change them if needed. The primary objective of the POS is to emphatically state what's in scope and what's out of scope for the project.

Once the key POS elements are defined and documented, the project should immediately transition to the planning phase of the project life cycle.

Project Planning Workshop

The Project Planning Workshop (PPW) is a structured meeting designed to define the activities and resources that will be necessary to fulfill the deliverables of the project. Benefits of conducting such a workshop include:

- Establishing a communication device whereby subject matter experts determine the necessary steps to deliver the project

- Applying organizational expertise and experience to further define the project
- Establishing ownership of the activities/tasks of the project plan.

The ultimate goals of the PPW include gathering the information necessary to create a project schedule and a project resource plan. In other words, the key question the team will answer is, "How do we do it?"

The intent of the workshop is to get experts to tell you what activities are required, who is going to do them, and when. The PIW agenda is designed to engage participants in detailed planning activities and allows you to obtain organizational buy-in to what needs to be done to successfully deliver the project.

As with the PIW, the PPW requires preparation. The meeting must be held with a defined agenda, clear meeting goals, review of prior (PIW) documentation, and organized meeting materials. Using the POS as the foundation, a typical PPW agenda might look like figure 2-2.

The process steps can be consistently applied to all projects, regardless of type or size:

1. Review deliverables
2. Define activities
3. Sequence activities
4. Estimate activity durations   ⟶   Repeat these steps for each deliverable!
5. Determine personnel resources
6. Create project schedule
7. Create project resource plan.

Successful meeting outcomes require disciplined meeting management techniques and keen facilitation skills. More details are provided in chapter 8.

	<Team or Project Name> **Project Planning Workshop Agenda** *<Logistics: Date, Time, Location, Call-In Numbers>*		
Duration	**Agenda Topic**	**Who**	**Goal**
	Introductions, workshop purpose/goals, review agenda and ground rules		Understand why we are here and the workshop approach
	Project risks, assumptions, issues, and decisions will be simultaneously captured		*Document and track important elements of the project*
	Project purpose— overview of project opportunity statement		Set context for detailed planning
	Step 1: Review deliverables		Understand deliverables
	The next set of steps will be used for each deliverable in the project		
	Step 2: Define activities/ tasks to meet each deliverable		Identify work necessary for each deliverable
	Step 3: Sequence activities/ tasks (i.e., build the network diagram)		Determine when each task must be performed in relation to other tasks
	Step 4: Estimate task/ activity duration		Determine the length of time to perform each task
	Step 5: Determine personnel resource skills		Identify the skills necessary to perform each task
	Perform the steps below after the deliverables have gone through steps 2–5		
	Step 6: Create project schedule		The data entry portion of this step can be performed during the meeting or off-line

Figure 2-2 Example of a PPW Agenda

	Step 7: Create project resource plan		Identify and document personnel resources names and skills required to complete project work
	Step 8: Create project communications plan		Identify and document the project stakeholders, their communication needs, and the management methods
	At the end of the session		
	Next steps: Assign owners and due dates		Identify who owns what and when it is due
	Meeting evaluation		Workshop evaluation and how to improve it

Figure 2-2 Example of a PPW Agenda (*Continued*)

TEAM CHARTER

Once the project has been clearly defined, remaining team members are recruited. This is the time to define the team goals, often referred to as the team charter. The objective of clarifying team goals is to turn a group into a team. Remember, the difference between a team and a group is that team members are interdependent for overall performance. Teams require clarity about purpose, goals, or work products and also need more discipline in hammering out a common working approach. A "real" team also establishes collective accountability and has true interdependencies among team members and real shared accountability.

The challenge for many project teams is knowing the advantages obtained in defining team goals versus the investment required. In other words, how much time is really needed to declare team objectives in order for the team to successfully operate as a true team?

I'm not a big fan of project team charters because I've found that often they are too cumbersome to create, manage, and use to effect team unity. However, I do like the intent of the charter. A team charter defines a team's purpose, approach, and infrastructure while carrying out the project. It is typically a team-oriented document that also includes guidelines on behavior, administrative functions, and relationships. It is designed to allow team members who are otherwise unfamiliar with their peers on the team to be aware of team expectations and their role within the team dynamic.

Too often, however, project teams become entrenched in the documentation of a lengthy team charter, which team members seldom refer to during the life of the project. In fact, many teams find themselves challenged in creating a charter simply because most team members cannot agree on what information should or should not be incorporated into the document. In other instances, project managers exercise excessive authoritative power, forcing team members to comply with their view on how the project *should* perform.

In the spirit of vanilla, keep it simple: Address only what is absolutely necessary to keep your team on track, and engage all team members in the process. The primary reason for clarifying team goals is to make sure everyone on the team understands two interrelated needs—the project goals and the team goals.

The team charter should be developed during team formation. The project team leader typically takes the lead to draft the team purpose, team behaviors, team membership, and team meeting schedule. Team members must be allowed to comment and adjust the charter to appropriately reflect all team member's input.

To keep the process easy and effective, establish team goals by including minimal elements in the project charter:

- *Team purpose.* Specify why the team is being created. To make the purpose statement more concrete, ask "What is the final product of this team?" Include a short list of team responsibilities to establish clarity and support the team's mission.

- *Team behaviors.* Determine the "right" set of behaviors to support productive teamwork. Ideally, the set of team behaviors should exist in a generic form for all teams within the same organization; it is the best way to drive cultural adoption of teamwork across the enterprise.
- *Team roster.* Identify who is on the team including title, contact information, and preferred mode of communication.
- *Team meeting schedule.* Establish when the team will meet, the frequency of the meetings, where the meetings will be held, and the duration of the meetings.

Although this might sound like oversimplification to some, I suggest that the simpler your targets, the more likely you are to reach them. Always challenge yourself and your team members by asking, "Will this information potentially minimize conflict or confusion later in the project or on our team?" If the answer is "yes," the information probably should be incorporated into the team goals. The team charter template (figure 2-3) might help.

Many project team charters include additional elements, but be careful. As you add additional pieces of information to the charter, you will slow down the team and divert its focus from achieving its project objectives. Don't waste a lot of time creating a lengthy charter, only to have team members file it away to collect dust.

It is also worth mentioning that the length of the project will help define team goals. One of the most powerful actions a group can take on behalf of itself and the project is to determine what type of team is needed to best serve the needs of the project. Then the group can proceed with appropriate planning for its own development in concert with what the project needs it to be and with an investment of developmental resources appropriate for the possible return.

Make your team real by making your team charter real. Document the team mission and distribute it to team members.

What It Is

A team charter defines a team's purpose, approach, and infrastructure while carrying out the project.

Why It's Useful

The team charter provides guidelines on behavior, administrative functions, and relationships among team members. It is designed to allow team members who are otherwise unfamiliar with their peers on the team to be aware of team expectations and their role within the team dynamic.

How to Use It

Use the team charter to formalize the group as a team, align team members' expectations, and rally team members around a common goal.

Team Charter

Team Name:_____

Team Purpose:_____

_____

Team Behaviors:_____

_____

_____

_____

Team Roster:

Name	Title	Company/Department	Contact Information

Figure 2-3 Team Charter Template

Team Meeting Schedule:

Date	Time	Location	Call-in

Approved By:_____

Figure 2-3 Team Charter Template (*Continued*)

Figure 2-4 is an example of how simple, yet effective, a team charter can be.

Because there are a wide variety of teams, team sizes, and organizational protocols, no two team charters will look the same. Therefore, team members have a great deal of latitude in determining what information should or should not be included in the charter. Keep the process succinct and engage all team members in the process.

It's important that all team members be involved because the team charter formalizes information that is frequently known as "understood" among team members. Some team members (especially those

Purpose

The NP project team develops the project plan and budget in order to achieve the project goal. Once plans and budgets are approved, the NP project team is responsible for implementing the plan. Additionally, the NP project team will consistently communicate project activities and alert project stakeholders to issues impeding project success as soon as identified.

Major responsibilities

- Determines work breakdown
- Determines resource needs
- Performs work
- Reports estimates to complete
- Reports work progress

Team Administration

All project documents will be stored in the shared folder, labeled "NP Project Team." All project scope documents, project plans, project status reports, resource grids, and communication plans will be housed in individual files. Each document will use XXX version control. Project status reports will be submitted via the XYZ project portal; the project manager is responsible for submitting each weekly report.

Membership

List members and contact information here.

Meeting Frequency

Every Monday beginning April 1, 2010, 9 a.m.–11 a.m., until project close.

Charter Acceptance

Figure 2-4 New Product Project Team Charter

who have participated in many charter exercises in the past) might balk at the notion that they should participate. Try to engage all team members so everyone has an equal stake in the team's success.

Because most team charters have little or no enforcement associated with them, the success of the charter frequently hinges on the team members' verbal acceptance of the words on the paper. One way to encourage adherence is to ask each team member to sign the team charter. There is still no real way to formally enforce what's written, but team members who sign a charter are usually more likely to adhere to the agreement.

Most organizations rely on teamwork to get the job done. This is especially true for projectized organizations. Yet despite the prevalence of teamwork, most teams muddle along during the life of the project in the absence of a team charter, hoping team dynamics will improve as the project progresses from one phase to the next.

Launching the team with a team charter is an easy, effective way to formalize the group as a team, align team member expectations, and rally members around a common team goal. The next critical step, addressed in chapter 3, is to implement supporting behaviors.

Implementing Supporting Behaviors

The quality of our expectations determines the quality of our actions.

—Andre Godin

Determining the "right" set of behaviors to support productive teamwork in never easy because team dynamics are intricate and difficult. Ideally, a set of behaviors to best support teamwork must be articulated in a universal language because these behaviors need to be owned by the entire organization, not just project teams. When team behaviors are set at the enterprise level, their introduction sets the framework for ensuring the behaviors are a means of conducting business, not just a set of words hung along corporate walls. Ideally, the entire organization must believe in the power of teamwork to experience improvements in project outcomes and operational performance as a result of strong teamwork.

To successfully define team behaviors, create a set of team behaviors that use simple language, apply to the organizational culture, and can be easily understood and practiced. No matter how large or small the organization, all team behaviors must be clear and comprehensible to all staff, regardless of position or title. Organizations are more likely to realize results if they establish straightforward behaviors directly related to improving team dynamics.

Create measurable behaviors so staff can easily be held accountable. Accountability can be achieved when team leaders (and ultimately team members) are held accountable in a valid way. This can be achieved through specific performance targets when expressed in measurable ways.

In recognition of the value of cross-functional teamwork, organizations should reinforce a set of team behaviors that can be adopted by all teams in the organization regardless of size, purpose, or duration. The behaviors should be derived to guide how teams operate and achieve successful team results. Ultimately, organizations that create a standard set of behaviors to support team dynamics will improve decision-making, enhance efficiencies, and promote better business results.

To establish an organizational culture in support of teamwork, the behaviors should ideally be created by the Chief Executive Officer. At the very least, the behaviors must be endorsed by the CEO in order to achieve sustained existence. If team behaviors have not been established as part of the corporate culture, you, as the project manager, may set the tone among your project team members. This is not ideal, but it can be done.

In 2002, Harvard Pilgrim Health Care (HPHC) CEO Charlie Baker recommended a set of expected behaviors for management and staff. This was right around the time the dust had begun to settle after the organization's turnaround. Up until this point, Baker hadn't spent any time at all thinking about appropriate standards of behavior—the company had been in crisis, focused on staying in business.

The behaviors were designed according to Baker's own views about what constitutes appropriate behavior and team interactions; they were designed to help facilitate cross-functional teamwork. The set of behaviors was introduced to HPHC staff as a means of transitioning staff from an open culture to a synchronous culture. The behaviors reinforced a very simple, yet compelling theory: Organizations do much of their work through groups; groups tend to be complex challenges from a management and communications view; and if the company could come up with some ways to improve team dynamics, it could enhance group performance.

EXPECTED BEHAVIORS FOR TEAMWORK

A set of team behaviors promote TEAMwork:

- **T**reat each other with dignity and respect.
- **E**xchange the needs and impacts of your work with others.
- **A**ctively seek and receive feedback for improvement.
- **M**ake timely decisions and solve problems quickly.

These behaviors are based on HPHC's original behaviors, with adjustments made over time. Teams value these behaviors because they are simply stated and easy to understand. They also have a universal appeal, regardless of team size or corporate culture.

Over the past four years, these behaviors have been introduced to other companies as a way to emphasize and promote healthy team dynamics. Regardless of corporate environment, team size, or industry type, this set of behaviors is a comfortable way to promote the value of cross-functional teamwork. Those who have adopted these TEAMwork behaviors believe the behaviors have had a positive impact on project (and other) team results.

Let's take a closer look at each behavior.

Treat Each Other with Dignity and Respect

We all want to be treated well. But in today's business environment, where we are forced to produce at a frenzied pace and do more with less, we sometimes lash out at others when we are "up against it." Regardless of the circumstances, we must always act in a dignified manner, treating everyone with respect. When you maintain your dignity in even the most trying of circumstances, you'll find that you'll be better able to build and maintain professional relationships.

It's important to make sure that all of our dealings with others are meant to benefit each other and not take advantages of weaknesses and vulnerabilities. Ethical behavior, dignity, and respect are the hallmarks of interpersonally competent people. True team players never seek to get even; they find ways to build creative solutions out of conflict, disagreement, and disappointment.

Exchange the Needs and Impacts of Your Work with Others

Exchange relationships among team members are critical to team success. A team that is able to coordinate its actions is more likely to achieve its shared goal. However, the nature of project work is changing. We work in more complex business environments with more interactions with unknown team members. Today's challenges require that teams have strong cross-collaboration, seamless connections, and a thorough understanding of what each team member brings to the table.

Team members must support and promote intra- and inter-departmental teamwork and consistently share knowledge and information. Every new team should launch with a set of guiding questions to promote collaboration and communication:

- What's happening?
- What's new?
- Who knows what?
- How do I share information with others?

The level of exchange among team members determines team success. Team members who openly and freely exchange information and who understand the impacts of their actions (or lack thereof) on other team members often acquire the skills and knowledge needed to drive complex projects forward according to scope, schedule, and budget.

Actively Seek and Receive Feedback for Improvement

Feedback is an essential skill in interpersonal communication; the quality of one's ability to give and receive feedback influences all kinds of relationships. Giving and receiving feedback is not a comfortable practice for most people. We're unsure who to ask for feedback, how to ask for it, and what to do with it once we receive it.

For many, feedback occurs once a year during the annual performance review process. Feedback is often submitted anonymously, and in many cases there is no documentation to support the ratings. Without specific examples, the receiver of the information is at a disadvantage. Real examples provide information that is actionable; without the details, how can anyone respond to the feedback in a real and meaningful way?

Make Timely Decisions and Solve Problems Quickly

There's an old samurai saying that goes something like this: "No decision should take longer than the time required to draw seven breaths." Problem solving and decision-making are important skills for business and life. In today's frenetic business environment, there is often little time to waste. Making prompt decisions and taking swift action are skills that are required to succeed.

THE VALUE OF TEAMWORK

Creating a set of expected behaviors to support TEAMwork sets the foundation for achieving better business outcomes. But staff can't buy into the new behaviors unless they really understand them and interpret them in a similar manner. Alan Slobodnik, cofounder of Options for Change, assisted HPHC with the development and understanding of its expected behaviors. Alan and Deborah Slobodnik are consultants and trainers who specialize in organizational change. Their practical method for intervening in human systems on the behavioral level guided HPHC through the identification and implementation of its Expected Behaviors.[1]

The Slobodniks believe successful organizations must invest time and energy to bring about true changes in behavior. "Organizations must go the extra mile to ensure the 'right' behaviors are both reflective of the corporate culture and deeply embedded in it," states Alan. Companies that require the use of expected behaviors on project teams and corporate committees and that have embedded them in their HR systems so team members are held accountable for fulfilling the behaviors in a real and measurable way have seen dramatic results in team and business output.

Much of the material in this book has been introduced to staff who rely on teamwork to achieve project and business outcomes. Those who have adopted the expected behaviors as a means of doing business and interacting with one another say the behaviors have had an enormous impact on both team morale and team results.

IMPLEMENTING AND PROMOTING EXPECTED BEHAVIORS

Once team behaviors are defined, it is important to implement the behaviors across your team and to promote their adoption among team members. The primary goal is to publicly promote expected behaviors to team members and get team member feedback on the behaviors so everyone on the team has a general understanding of the behaviors and a heightened awareness of the behaviors during team interactions. It's critical that all team members buy in to the behaviors so everyone has a vested interest in making them real.

To ensure both awareness and accountability, all project teams should go through a series of stage-gate activities in support of the expected behaviors. Project teams that participate in a minimal set of activities and tool use have favorable results on a consistent basis. The required set of activities includes the team leader's knowing what to look for in the group, a structured team conversation on expected behaviors, the completion of an expected behaviors survey, and a rules of engagement exercise. Let's look at each in detail.

Key Group Elements

In virtually all groups, there are two primary elements—content and purpose. Content focuses on the goal or tasks on which the group is working. Process, on the other hand, is what happens between and among group members while the group is in place. Also known as team dynamics, it's all about emotional elements such as team morale, level of participation among team members, styles of influence, leadership struggles, conflict, competition, cooperation, etc. Think of the two elements as the yin and yang of project teams. Content includes the "technical" elements, and purpose focusing on the "human" elements.

As team leader, it is important that you consider both content and process during team creation and throughout the group's tenure. Ironically, in most team interactions, very little attention is paid to process, even when it is the major cause of inefficient team interaction. Being sensitive to group process will allow you, as the team leader, to diagnose group problems early and deal with them more effectively.

There are a few key areas to focus on while evaluating team dynamics. Consider team participation, levels and styles of member influence, how decisions are made (or not), and general team atmosphere.

The Group Guide (see figure 3-1) provides guidelines to help you quickly analyze your team's behavior. It is most helpful when used during the early stage of team formation. The first two months of team

What It Is

The Group Guide helps team leaders to observe, note, and analyze group dynamics.

Why It's Useful

Sensitivity to group process will enable the team leader to diagnose group problems early and deal with them more effectively. Awareness of group dynamics will enhance the team leader's worth to the group and enable him or her to be a more effective team leader, ultimately improving the team's ability to engage in productive group interactions and produce useful output.

How it Works

The guide prompts you to observe and consider team interactions and behaviors, helping you assess team dynamics.

Group Guide

Verbal Participation	One indication of team member involvement (or lack thereof) is verbal participation. Look for differences in participation among team members.
• Who are the high/low participators?	
• Are there certain times during a regular meeting when there are shifts in participation, e.g., high participators become quiet, low participators become talkative?	
• How much verbal exchange occurs that is not directly related to the agenda item or the topic of discussion?	

Figure 3-1 Group Guide

• Who talks to whom? Are there any patterns for a particular subgroup's interaction?	
• Are significant discussions occurring outside the team?	
Active Participation	Another kind of participation is active participation. Again, consider the differences among team members.
• Who attends meetings regularly?	
• Who arrives to meetings on time and is prepared?	
• Who attends a meeting but is not actively engaged, i.e., is doing something else?	
• Who arrives at a meeting, only to consistently excuse himself or herself mid-meeting to attend to "urgent" matters?	
Member Influence	Influence and participation are not the same. Some people might speak very little but still command attention; others might talk a lot but generally not be heard by others.
• Which members are high/low influencers?	
• How do high/low influencers capture the attention of others?	
• Do you observe any shifts in influence? If so, when and why?	
• Do you see any rivalry in the group? Struggles for control?	

Figure 3-1 Group Guide (*Continued*)

• Do you see anyone attempting to force his or her will or values on other group members or trying to bully them to support his or her position or opinion?	
• Do you have passive members on the team? Are they always eager to support other group members' decisions?	
Decision-making	Many types of decisions are made on project teams every day. Often, decisions are made on teams with little consideration given to the effects of the decisions on other team members, project stakeholders, or other, interdependent projects.
• Does anyone try to include everyone all the time, preventing the team from moving forward unless full team consensus is reached?	
• Does anyone on the team make self-authorized decisions, i.e., never soliciting input from others?	
• Are there individuals who consistently push decisions through over other team members?	
• How often does the group drift from the issue at hand or jump from topic to topic, preventing timely decisions?	

Figure 3-1 Group Guide (*Continued*)

Team Atmosphere	The way in which the team operates and interacts will by default establish a team atmosphere. Consider the atmosphere that the team has created.
• Has the team created a friendly atmosphere?	
• Is the atmosphere stressful? Is there constant conflict among team members?	
• Are team members consistently engaged, involved, and interested?	
• Can you identify emotional trends in the group? For example, do you observe anger, frustration, excitement, enthusiasm?	
• Do team members laugh, have fun, and enjoy one another?	

Figure 3-1 Group Guide (*Continued*)

engagement should provide you, the team leader, with enough exposure to team dynamics to adequately analyze group behavior.

As team leader, it is important to look for these elements during early team formation. Having sensitivity and awareness to group process early will better enable you to diagnose team problems early and deal with them more effectively. These early observations will also allow you to plan and engage in a discussion with your team about the impact and value of adopting TEAM behaviors as a way to enhance team effectiveness.

TEAM Talk Guide

The TEAM Talk Guide assists team leaders in planning a discussion with their team about the impact and value of adopting TEAM behaviors as a way to enhance team effectiveness. The tool and process is adapted from FasTeams®, a set of tools and processes designed by Options for Change to help team leaders create the culture and behaviors needed to accomplish work more efficiently.[2] The intent behind the TEAM Talk Guide is to guide the project manager through a discussion with his or her team to evaluate which behaviors are done well and identify where and how improvements can be made.

Engaging team members in this discussion is not as difficult as you might expect. The key to having successful dialogue is timing—when to have such a conversation defines success more often than the actual change itself. Timing is critical. Teams should not conduct this discussion too early; a group needs some time to cohere as a team before being able to evaluate its ability to behave well. On the other hand, don't wait too long because bad behavior is hard to change. Experience suggests that a successful dialogue for project teams should occur during the first three months of team formation. Obviously, this timeline needs to be adjusted for teams with abbreviated project start/end dates.

The project manager (team leader) starts the discussion by setting the context. The intent is to have the team leader initiate a conversation that guides the team to evaluate those team behaviors that are done well and identify where and how improvements could be made.

It is important to reinforce the value of team behaviors from the leader's perspective. The leader should express personal commitment to team behaviors and acknowledge that even leaders don't always get them "right." The leader must give the team members permission to hold each other accountable, including the leader. The team leader must actively seek input from each team member as to whether the leader is demonstrating TEAM behaviors. Sharing the idea that all team members must hold each other accountable to demonstrate these behaviors is critical.

It also falls on you, as the team leader, to remain committed to the behaviors as you guide the project from start to finish. Project leadership buy-in and endorsement are what make team behaviors work. Credible endorsement relies on sincere actions, and believable actions can occur only if team leaders live the behaviors.

Team leaders set the tone for team interactions; team members learn through example. If you as the team leader don't believe it's necessary to invest in team dynamics to produce productive results, then don't bother. You must practice what you preach to create true team harmony. The waterfall effect applies. Project sponsors should also believe in the value of team dynamics. The trickle-down effect is powerful and real. Team leadership can make or break a true team culture.

This is a great opportunity to set the context for the group and to focus a conversation on the importance of strong team dynamics. It is also a terrific occasion for team leaders to get a preliminary read on team members. An initial dialogue, even in an abbreviated fashion, will provide a glimpse into team member sentiments. A team member who rolls his eyes, for example, might be a team member who is predictably more difficult to get on board compared to his colleagues. Conversely, a team member who responds to the initial dialogue with enthusiasm and appreciation for strong team dynamics might become one of your strongest advocates.

A preliminary dialogue between the team leader and team members will provide some interesting insights. A successful team leader will be able to introduce a discussion around the importance of strong team dynamics and observe team member response and reaction to the preliminary discussion to better prepare and plan the next steps in redefining team behaviors.

The initial discussion regarding team behaviors does not need to be lengthy to be effective. Dedicate the last 20 minutes in a future meeting to having this conversation. By scheduling the item on a future meeting agenda, you are making a conscious effort to give the discussion importance. It also allows team members to transition from their regular team business to this topic in a focused way.

At the conclusion of this dialogue, team members should have a clear understanding of the importance of high-performing teams, recognize the team leader's commitment to guiding the team to achieving a higher level of team interaction, and anticipate the opportunity for ongoing team engagement throughout the process.

The TEAM Talk Guide is presented in figure 3-2.

TEAM Assessment Survey

A great next step in the process is to have team members assess their team's current adherence to TEAM behaviors. This can be done in a number of ways. The easiest and most successful way to collect this feedback is by survey. All team members are asked to take a TEAM assessment survey, which is a simple and anonymous way for members to assess their ability to behave according to expectations. The survey might look like the example in figure 3-3.

In today's environment, surveys can be administered in many different ways to encourage team member input. Large organizations often have survey-tool capability in their marketing department; more often than not, marketing will be happy to assist you. For other organizations, web-based survey tools are inexpensive and easy to design. Not only are they simple to use, but they also can be submitted anonymously, further encouraging team member participation. Web-based surveys allow you to easily track response rate and trend results. Websites such as *SurveyMonkey.com*, *SurveyGizmo.com*, and *QuestionPro.com* offer easy-to-use survey tools.

What It Is

Team Talk helps team leaders have a discussion with their team about the impact and value of adopting TEAM behaviors as a way to enhance team effectiveness and project outcomes. The intent is to have the team leader initiate a discussion that guides the team to evaluate those behaviors that are done well and identify where and how improvements could be made.

Why It's Useful

Engaging the team in a discussion about the value of TEAM behaviors allows all team members to identify and discuss best practices and lessons learned to support healthy team dynamics. This is a terrific opportunity to share previous experiences, including experiences that resulted in both positive and negative outcomes. Team leaders who have this input from team members early in team formation are more likely to identify team strengths and team weaknesses, which will allow leaders to best leverage team members to serve project needs.

How It Works

TEAM Talk helps you set the context with your team on the importance of team dynamics, particularly from your (the team leader's) perspective. By setting the stage as the team leader, you also need to engage all team members, so all voices are heard. The process contains four steps:

1. Set the stage with a preliminary team discussion: *Why are we talking about our team?*
2. Assess TEAM behaviors: *How are we doing as a team?*
3. Identify which behavior(s) will be chosen for improvement, and gain team commitment: *How can we improve?*
4. Identify an improvement approach and improvement timelines and metrics: *How do we make our team stronger, more effective?*

Figure 3-2 TEAM Talk Guide

TEAM Talk Guide

Topic	Comments
1. Set the stage *Why are we talking about our team?*	Set the context by reinforcing the value of TEAMwork from your perspective. • As a team leader, you should express your belief that strong teams produce better outcomes. • State your commitment to demonstrate TEAM behaviors, and acknowledge that you won't always follow through perfectly and will expect the team to hold you accountable. • State that you want everyone to hold each other accountable for demonstrating these behaviors, too.
2. Assess TEAM behaviors *How are we doing as a team?*	Explain the process so all team members understand how the group will promote team dynamics. • Allow each member the opportunity to state his or her position on the value of teamwork and why it is/is not important. • Each member takes the TEAM assessment survey (Figure 3-3).
3. Identify behavior(s) for improvement, and gain team commitment *How can we improve?*	Based on the team survey, identify your team's strengths and opportunities. • Identify which behaviors are currently being practiced well. • Identify which behaviors will be chosen for improvement and discuss improvement strategies.

Figure 3-2 TEAM Talk Guide (*Continued*)

4. Identify an improvement approach *How do we make our team stronger and more effective?*	Review associated tools in tool kit and determine whether any are appropriate for the team's use. • Identify action items, owners, and due dates. • Determine performance metrics.

Figure 3-2 TEAM Talk Guide (*Continued*)

What It Is

The TEAM assessment survey is a list of survey questions intended to help team members assess how they are behaving as a group and according to TEAM behaviors.

Why It's Useful

Allowing team members the opportunity to assess team dynamics in an anonymous way will provide honest feedback on how the group is performing as a team. The results of the survey can guide the team in identifying which behavior(s) need improvement and what to do to enhance team results.

How It Works

Distribute the survey questions to all team members, and provide a deadline for when responses are due. Collect and tally the results, and present them to the team for discussion and next steps.

TEAM Assessment Survey

Based on your experience and observations to date, how well do you believe our team is performing in the following areas? Select the best rating for each statement.

Figure 3-3 TEAM Assessment Survey

1. Relationships are authentic and respectful.				
Extremely Weak 1	Fairly Weak 2	Neutral 3	Fairly Strong 4	Extremely Strong 5

2. Members support and promote intra- and inter-departmental teamwork.				
Extremely Weak 1	Fairly Weak 2	Neutral 3	Fairly Strong 4	Extremely Strong 5

3. Members feel good about their positive impact on others and the good they do for the organization.				
Extremely Weak 1	Fairly Weak 2	Neutral 3	Fairly Strong 4	Extremely Strong 5

4. Members are sensitive to how their actions, ideas, or contributions will impact the workload of others on the team.				
Extremely Weak 1	Fairly Weak 2	Neutral 3	Fairly Strong 4	Extremely Strong 5

5. Members explore differences with enthusiasm and welcome healthy debate.				
Extremely Weak 1	Fairly Weak 2	Neutral 3	Fairly Strong 4	Extremely Strong 5

6. Team is effective in making timely decisions.				
Extremely Weak 1	Fairly Weak 2	Neutral 3	Fairly Strong 4	Extremely Strong 5

7. Members actively seek out opinions and feedback from each other.				
Extremely Weak 1	Fairly Weak 2	Neutral 3	Fairly Strong 4	Extremely Strong 5

8. Members freely and openly discuss ideas and suggestions on how to improve. Opinions and advice are frequently solicited and shared among members.				
Extremely Weak 1	Fairly Weak 2	Neutral 3	Fairly Strong 4	Extremely Strong 5

9. The team leader is perceived as a partner who actively engages all team members and guides the team toward a shared goal.				
Extremely Weak 1	Fairly Weak 2	Neutral 3	Fairly Strong 4	Extremely Strong 5

Figure 3-3 TEAM Assessment Survey (*Continued*)

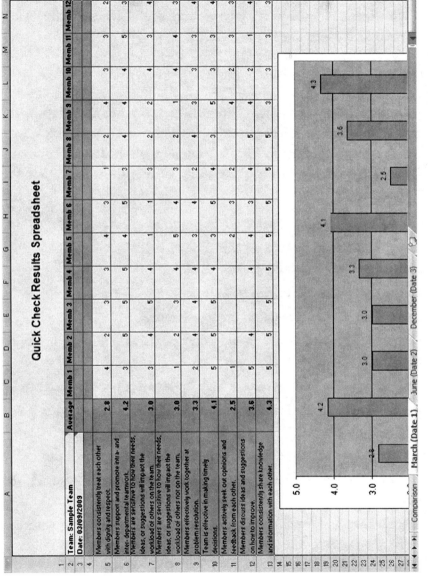

Figure 3-4 Survey Results Spreadsheet

For those who opt for the old-fashioned way or who have a small team, there is a simple Excel-based tool included in your tool kit. It is an easy template to help you collect and track survey results and share them with team members. It's particularly useful when dealing with smaller teams. It looks like figure 3-4.

TEAM Discussions

Regardless of how you solicit and collect team member input, it's important to share the team results with the team and talk about what the results might mean for the team as a whole. Once the survey results are in, the team can use a number of questions to initiate the team discussion:

- How do TEAM behaviors impact our group's effectiveness?
- Survey data show that we do this TEAM behavior well. What does performing "well" look like?
- How can we promote TEAM behaviors?
- Do any TEAM behaviors need improvement?
- What does it look like when we don't perform a TEAM behavior well?
- What needs to happen to make it "safe" to give feedback to each other?
- How will we communicate to each other if a TEAM behavior is not being exhibited?
- Why should we improve TEAM behaviors? What's in it for us?
- How will we know when we are successfully practicing a TEAM behavior?
- Are we willing to try using a support tool to help us improve our use of a TEAM behavior?
- How and when will we evaluate the usefulness of the tool?
- How frequently should we reevaluate our ability to practice TEAM behaviors?

Always take time to identify and acknowledge the behaviors the team performs well. It is human nature for us to immediately focus on the low areas of performance, resulting in the group's feeling less than adequate about how they are performing as a group. Spend a few minutes to congratulate the team on what works well. This is a terrific way to keep team members positive and effectively maintain the balance between what behaviors work well for the team versus what might need improvement.

It is important to allow all team members to share their opinion and react to the survey results. This is important for a number of reasons. First, it builds engagement among all team members and does not play favorites (those who have the loudest voice). Second, it enables survey participants to explain why they answered a particular question the way they did. This is very important.

In the case of one team that recently took the survey, the initial results appeared to score very low across a number of questions. After further discussion, however, team members realized they had interpreted the question differently, causing a number of participants to answer the survey question contrary to how they would have had they understood the question in the same way as the other team members.

Remember that keeping survey questions simple will reduce misinterpretation among team members; ideally, talking about results will eliminate confusion.

The results of the team's discussion will determine next steps. If a team has much opportunity for improvement, the team leader must work with the team to prioritize areas of pain. The best way to realize success is through team engagement and agreement. In other words, the team leader is responsible for guiding the discussion and fostering agreement among team members regarding which areas to focus on and the tactics needed to reach improvement. The team leader should not mandate actions based on his or her opinions or philosophies; this approach does not foster engagement among the group.

The goal of this discussion is to allow each member on the team to discuss the meaning of TEAM behaviors from an individual and team perspective; identify which behavior(s) will be chosen for improvement and gain group commitment; develop an improvement approach, a timeline, and metrics; and confirm next steps.

The survey is a good way to obtain a baseline measurement of the team's ability to work well together. When the survey is done anonymously, participants are more inclined to answer honestly. Once a team has baseline results, it is ready to acknowledge its strengths and tackle areas where improvement is needed.

The survey is also a great way to track and record a team's progress over time. Teams should wait six to eight months before taking a second survey. Project teams have constraints around this; if the project team is in place for less than six months, there really isn't time to conduct a follow-up survey.

This model works very well for long-term teams because it provides a chronological view of team growth and development. Because long-standing teams sometimes experience degradation in results as the project progresses through various phases, the survey process is a great way to catch early warning signs.

Surveys should also be considered at other key points for a team. A significant turnover in team membership, for example, is a good time to reassess survey results because such an event can dramatically affect the team's character and ability to work well together.

It is also important for teams to set realistic goals when identifying which behaviors warrant improvement. Keep your action plan very focused on just a few prioritized areas of need. Regardless of how needy a team might be, it must maintain a balance between improving the team environment and meeting project deliverables. Teams that take on too much at once will not succeed in either effort, resulting in universal disaster.

For teams that are up against tight timelines and don't have the luxury to formally solicit and assess team member feedback, there are other ways to quickly collect member input through easier processes.

After the results are in and the team has had an opportunity to discuss them is a great time to conduct a rules of engagement exercise.

RULES OF ENGAGEMENT

Conducting a Rules of Engagement conversation will allow team members to develop an initial contract that describes how they will treat each other with dignity and respect. Since the meanings of *dignity* and *respect* vary from person to person, this tool will help the team identify and discuss the various elements of behavior that are critical to the success of ongoing interactions. Adapted here with permission from Options for Change, this is perhaps the most valuable tool in the tool kit.[3] In fact, if you decide to use only one tool to enhance team dynamics, this is *the* tool to use.

The Rules of Engagement exercise focuses on six key areas of behavior:

- Basic courtesies
- Operating agreement
- Problem-solving and decision-making
- Accountability
- Conflict resolution
- Leader's role.

In a team meeting, schedule extra time to focus on this. If a team does not dedicate time to this exercise, it will never happen. Many teams schedule a special session dedicated solely to rules of engagement. In this meeting, the team members brainstorm and record a list of key behaviors that are important to them and that best support operating agreements.

To start the exercise, consider asking questions such as "How do you like to work?" and "What is your work style?" and "What strengths do you bring?" Allow time for discussion of the key areas and behaviors that the team wants to adopt. Ensure that all voices are heard.

Run through each of the six key areas; all are important. However, teams might find that not all have equal weight. For example, conflict resolution might be more important to the group than operating agreement. Focus on getting through all the areas while seeking common ground for consensus. Be sure to confirm that each area is complete before moving on.

A team leader might need to solicit input from quiet team members; not everyone will have the same voice. As facilitators, it is important that team leaders acknowledge others' contributions to the discussion before relating their own remarks. Never distort others' views in order to advance your own. To be successful, the results of this exercise must represent the team's collective input. It is not the team leader's opportunity to mandate behavioral requirements from team members or chastise individual team members who lack team decorum.

For some teams, having an unbiased, unattached person lead the rules of engagement discussion often frees all participants to share opinions in a safe environment. It also levels the field among participants, creating equity among team members during the rules of engagement exercise.

Once the group decides on the key areas of behavior, it documents its rules of engagement and posts them at every meeting as a reminder. The visual reminder is a good way to keep team members in active pursuit of improvement. I have seen some teams go to great lengths to keep team members reminded—in once instance, a large program team had laminated wallet cards produced! Depending on the duration of the team, the group can decide whether the agreement needs to be refreshed; often teams do not return to their agreement unless there are challenges in a particular area.

Project managers sometimes find the rules of engagement exercise difficult. It requires facilitation, one of those "soft skills" not often taught in the project management world. To successfully facilitate a rules of engagement discussion, project managers must guide the group so all members of the team are engaged in the discussion and own the results. Project managers cannot force the team to accept the leader's desires; to hold weight, the results need to be fully owned by all team members.

Successful facilitation is similar to successful project management. It requires a delicate balance between the art and science of reaching objectives. Keen facilitators have the ability to create and sequence questions that move a group from surface considerations into the depth of any topic. Good facilitation is about knowing how to guide a group to results without hampering emerging possibilities.

When people are face-to-face, they need to talk and to listen. When several people are involved, especially when they don't know each other or they disagree, getting the talking, listening, and deciding sequence is hard. Traditionally, work teams have relied on the person "in charge" to play a facilitative role. The team leader is successful in this role when he or she is able to remain unbiased and results-oriented.

While facilitating, listen carefully to others. Ask clarifying questions to further understand what someone is saying; it is better to ask than to interpret incorrectly. Remember that silence can speak volumes. Allowing some space between comments creates an opportunity for team members to digest what someone has said. This allows others to add to the previous comment or offer a slightly different view. Allowing silence to linger is never easy, but it is necessary to ensure full team collaboration.

Here are some key phrases to help facilitate the rules of engagement exercise:

- What I heard you say is... .
- Can you give us an example so we can better understand what you are saying?

- Do we all agree on this item?
- Does anyone have a different perspective to offer?
- Have we exhausted this category? Are we ready to move on?

Effective facilitators are able to elicit the group's best responses to the questions that involve appealing to the imagination and encouraging some boldness in responses. The leader has to involve the entire group, find ways to draw out the quieter folk, calm the hyperactive, and push each one in the group to play an active role in the dialogue.

A key role of the facilitator is to provide objectivity to the group process. Facilitators wear many hats throughout the process. One hat might belong to the orchestra conductor who finds harmony among the blend of different instruments, and the other might belong to the dispassionate referee who understands the importance of maintaining a neutral stance toward differing views and opinions.

All the while, the facilitator must be nimble. When the unexpected happens, the ability to react quickly, redirect the group, or in some instances fly by the seat of one's pants can make the difference between success and failure.

The results of a well-facilitated rules of engagement exercise might look something like figure 3-5.

For skeptics who perceive this activity as nonsense and a waste of time when there is constructive and important project work to deliver, keep this in mind: Teams that conduct this exercise indicate that they are positively affected by the experience. Communication and working relationships improve, and team members become more aware of their behavior toward others, more aware of others' roles, and better at seeing different points of view.

For example, while facilitating a discussion around basic courtesies, I refereed a lively debate between team members regarding the use

Basic Courtesies

- Limit Blackberry use to check *only* urgent or emergency messages; if an urgent message requires an urgent response, leave the room to respond.
- Don't interrupt while someone is speaking.
- Listen to and respect the viewpoint of others.
- Acknowledge all virtual members by name when they join the meeting.
- Hold no sidebar conversations.

Operating Agreements

- Arrive on time for the meeting.
- Distribute agenda and supporting materials two days in advance of meeting.
- Meetings will begin promptly at 1:05 pm and conclude at 2:55 pm.
- A scheduled bio-break will be incorporated into all agendas.
- If the conference call/web-conference connection is lost, the person who initiated the meeting will reinitiate the meeting.
- If we don't reach quorum, we cancel the meeting.
- Members will complete a meeting evaluation at the end of the last meeting each month.

Problem-Solving and Decision-Making

- Make a decision based on what is reasonable from a business perspective and what will solve the problem, rather than hold out for perfection.
- Focus on making the timeliest decision possible. Strive for a 24-hour turnaround; if necessary, follow up on issues off-line.

Figure 3-5 Rules of Engagement Worksheet

- Make decisions based on presentation of a combination of facts, experience, and judgment.
- The team will make consensus-driven decisions. When the team reaches its threshold of decision-making authority, the project sponsor will make all necessary decisions within 24 hours to support the ongoing needs of the project.

Accountability

- Team members are expected to attend all team meetings. If unable to attend, team members must inform the team leader in advance; an alternate representative must be identified.
- Team members must arrive at meetings informed and ready to conduct business as defined in agenda. All "homework" assignments will be delivered on time.
- All members share responsibility—no finger-pointing or blaming.
- The team leader holds self and others accountable.

Conflict Resolution

- Make the discussion about the business problem and not about people—don't hold back if conflict arises.
- Ensure the discussion remains on point and that it does not become tangential to the main topic.
- Listen to understand the other person's point of view before giving your own.
- If a conflict cannot be resolved within the meeting period, the issue will be taken off-line; an update on the resolution will be given to team members as required.

Figure 3-5 Rules of Engagement Worksheet (*Continued*)

Leader's Role

- Ensure the meeting is facilitated and sticks to the agenda and schedule.
- Ensure presenters are well prepared and on point.
- Facilitate meetings for productivity and effectiveness.
- Ensure all conference call equipment is available and working; confirm all virtual team members are connected and able to participate fully.

Figure 3-5 Rules of Engagement Worksheet (*Continued*)

of electronic devices during a team meeting. One team member was adamantly opposed to the use of cell phones and Blackberries. The other member defended her use of electronics by explaining her plight: She was from the IT department, and she traveled from meeting to meeting throughout the day. As a result, the only way she was able to respond to system-related crises was through her Blackberry.

As the conversation progressed, team members gained a greater sense of appreciation for what some of their teammates dealt with on a day-to-day basis and how individual roles differ among team members. As a result, this team successfully came up with a compromise they could live with: Rather than ban all electronic devices, they limited their use; necessary communications via Blackberry or cell phone had to occur outside the meeting room.

Don't worry about placing a team rule in the "right place." I have seen too many teams get stuck when members couldn't decide whether a suggestion belonged in basic courtesies or operating agreements. It doesn't matter. If the rule is important enough to be mentioned and most team members believe it belongs under the category you are currently discussing, simply document it and move on. For most teams, running through all six categories will create a comprehensive set of rules, regardless of where they land.

Teams say the exercise creates a more comfortable working environment. Meetings become more productive, and teams become more efficient in meeting deliverables. The big surprise for most team leaders is the realization that the activities are not time-consuming and do not slow work down, nor do they stifle team energy or limit lively and productive discussion.

The size of your team will determine how you conduct this exercise. If a project manager is leading a large program, with hundreds of staff assigned, a rules of engagement exercise can't be conducted in one sitting. For larger programs, there are creative ways to conduct this exercise. A leader might want to conduct it with core team members only. A team leader could develop a "trickle-down" system, whereby project managers assigned to each subteam are responsible for leading their own discussions.

Regardless of how a rules of engagement session is conducted, remember two key points: A team must have total engagement, and it must document its results to be effective.

Remember, all teams are different. Regardless of how many familiar faces are on your next project assignment, don't presume members will act as they did on the previous mission. All projects have unique goals, deadlines, and budgets. Team members will perform according to unique assignments. When faced with new, tighter deadlines or bigger responsibilities, for example, even the most team-spirited members might exhibit unexpected behaviors. Treat each new team as a fresh start, and conduct a rules of engagement discussion as part of every new team launch.

Teams that conduct a survey and carry out a rules of engagement exercise find that these have a powerful one-two impact. The survey tool easily identifies team strengths and weaknesses; the rules of engagement exercise enables the team to flag and fix team behavior smoothly. Taken together, this is an effective preventive course of treatment to ensure successful team dynamics.

However, not all project teams will have enough time to conduct both an assessment and a rules of engagement discussion. Many teams operate at a frenzied pace, having too little time to deliver project deliverables according to abbreviated deadlines.

Project managers must assess how to best introduce expected behaviors to a team and instinctively know how many steps to follow in the process. Although completing both the survey and the rules of engagement exercise is ideal, it is not always realistic. If necessary, adjust the process steps to meet your team's needs. Some teams skip the survey and move directly to the rules of engagement. Do whatever works best to meet both the goals of the project and the needs of the team.

Once the rules of engagement are in place, how do you make them real? The next chapter explores ways to hold team members accountable for fulfilling the team's desire to achieve success.

Notes

1 Harvard Pilgrim Health Care implemented a set of Expected Behaviors to all staff in 2002. The roll-out took two years to complete; Alan Slobodnik was a member of the project team responsible for introducing Expected Behaviors to Harvard Pilgrim Health Care staff.
2 FasTeams® offers over 60 tools that cover the spectrum of management issues, ranging from team launch to change management issues. For more information, see the Options for Change website at http://www. optionsforchange.com/ft1pg.html (accessed June 8, 2010).
3 For more information about Options for Change and Rules of Engagement, please visit the Options for Change website at www.optionsforchange.com (accessed June 8, 2010).

CHAPTER 4

Establishing Accountability

Unless you, as the team leader, discuss how you and others on your team will be held accountable for meeting team expectations, previous efforts are all for naught. True accountability is both individual and shared; individual contributions lead to team success. Team effectiveness is measured by the group's collective outcomes and ability to deliver the project successfully.

Accountability is a hot topic in business today. Lack of accountability costs corporate America tens of billions of dollars a year in terms of rework inefficiency, and workplace conflicts and misunderstandings. Without systematic accountability on a team, there is little chance of high performance.

When there is lack of accountability on project teams, non-performers thrive while the diligent staff members pick up the slack. Resentment infiltrates the group, communication among team members drops, and stress levels rise among everyone.

Some people think accountability means accepting responsibility when a project goes off course. True accountability involves taking ownership of your own work *and* recognizing that your work efforts also affect others. In today's fast-paced business environment, it is important to know how your contributions fit into the big picture.

True accountability on project teams means knowing what your individual role is, how it supports the needs of the project as a whole, and how the project supports the overarching strategy of the organization.

Simply "doing what you are told" prevents you from understanding the big picture and appreciating the value of your own individual contribution, as well as the contributions of your teammates.

Teams work best when everyone is focused on the same goal. On project teams, the focus must be multidimensional. In other words, all project team members must fully understand the project goal to be effective team members; they also need to understand how the project goal supports the organization's strategy. The real power of teamwork is realized when everyone understands the vision of the company *and* recognizes how the project supports that vision.

Project managers need to understand the correlation between individual projects and business strategy, and they need to communicate the relationship to project team members on a regular basis. This necessitates a lot of feedback and exchange of information between the team leader and team members.

For the organization's overall goals to be achieved, everyone on the team, regardless of title or role, should feel as if he or she owns an important piece of the process. Team leaders must help team members see what specific actions, behaviors, and deliverables will lead their project to successful outcomes, supporting corporate success.

THE MATRIX

Matrix management came about as organizations recognized that, in an increasingly complex business world, they needed to find both a balance between key drivers of their business and a more effective way to employ the skills and talents of individuals across their organization. Recognizing the power of collaboration and sharing, more and more organizations have embraced management systems that link both the vertical hierarchy and the horizontal relationship. In other words, many functional boundaries have blurred as more and more working relationships have been established where they are most needed and add the most value, with little regard to functional distinction or title.

Matrix management offers many benefits to organizations. A matrix structure can maximize individual skills while minimizing the burden on management. On the other hand, matrix structures put new pressures on those who run projects. Project managers have less control over team members who do not directly report to them. They are required to communicate more effectively. They need to introduce systems and processes that empower team members but do not hamper decision-making or stifle creativity.

The key behind successful matrix management is the ability to hold team members consistently accountable, regardless of reporting relationship. In other words, effective team leaders are able to instill responsibility and liability across the entire constituency, for the success of the project and the company.

Once the team has been defined, team goals have been clarified, and supporting team behaviors have been established, team members must be held accountable for fulfilling each requirement. Team leaders must take the lead to ensure that all individuals are linked through acceptance of responsibility and expectations. The linkage of the people on the team established by their accepting maximum accountability in order to fulfill the mission of the team is vital. One break in the chain and not only will the mission not be realized, but relationships will suffer.

All team leaders must take the time to express their performance expectations to all team members, regardless of what role they play on the team or their longevity as a team member. The objective is to define the expectation as the minimum acceptable performance level and get member commitment to strive for each expectation. The goal is to have all team members maximize their skills, do the best work they are capable of, and continue to learn and grow on the team.

THE ACCOUNTABILITY FACTOR

Teams are successful when they are action-oriented and when individual team members are accountable for delivering specific assignments according to assigned due dates. The RAID process was designed to ensure quick action. Originally using just easel sheets and markers, the process forced action by documenting action items, owners, and due dates during team meetings. Before the team meeting ended, the action items and dues dates were reviewed so everyone on the team understood what they owned and when it needed to be delivered.

The RAID template (see Figure 4-1) captures all **r**isks to be mitigated, **a**ssumptions to be validated, **i**ssues to be resolved and **d**ecisions to be documented. It tracks what action is needed and when it is due. The tool is a consolidated format that lets you record all RAID items in one central place rather than in three or four different documents. It was designed to create discipline and consistency in managing action items while launching and managing projects.

The Excel tool tracks what action is needed, who is doing it, when it is being done, and the status of the item. Not only does it impose prompt actions, but it also catalogues all issues identified throughout the life of the project. It can be easily sorted by "open/closed" items and "due dates," supporting action orientation and endorsing results. The RAID template should be introduced as soon as the project is initiated and it should be maintained throughout the project life cycle.

Figure 4-2 shows what the RAID template looks like.

IDENTIFY COMPETENCIES

Team leaders can hold team members accountable for performance and support growth by defining levels of expected performance for each team member. To keep it simple, identify a short list of competencies for each team member. Be sure to include both technical skills and team behaviors.

What It Is

The RAID template captures all risks to be mitigated, assumptions to be validated, issues to be resolved, and decisions to be documented. It tracks what action is needed, the owners, and due dates.

Why It's Useful

The tool is a consolidated format that lets you record all RAID items in one central place rather than in three or four different documents. It is designed to create discipline and consistency in managing action items across the team; it maintains action and instills accountability across team members. The Excel tool tracks what action is needed, who is doing it, when it is being done, and the status. Not only does it impose prompt action, but it also catalogues all issues identified throughout the life of the project. It can be easily sorted by "open/closed" items and "due dates," supporting action orientation and endorsing results.

How to Use It

The RAID template should be employed early in team formation and during project launch because having a central list of all risks, assumptions, issues, and decisions related to the project early provides a terrific audit trail in support of team activities. The RAID template should be introduced as soon as the project is initiated and should be maintained throughout the project life cycle.

For specific instructions and sorting options, refer to the "Help for This Tool" tab on the RAID tool.

When listing your RAID item(s), refer to the following key to appropriately catalogue each item:

R = Risk
A = Assumption
AI = Action Item
I = Issue
D = Decision

Figure 4-1 RAID Template

RAID (Risks, Assumptions, Issues, Decisions)

Sort & Renumber

ver. 2008.08.21

sorted by "open/closed", then "date due"

Seq #	UID	RAID Code	DESCRIPTION and IMPACT	DATE OPENED	OWNER	ACTION TO BE TAKEN / STATUS / RESOLUTION	DATE DUE	DATE CLOSED
1	2							
2	3							
3	1							
4	4							
5	5							
6	6							
7	7							
8	8							
9	9							

Figure 4-2 Example of RAID Template

The four-step process looks like this:

1. Define competencies.
2. Set expectations.
3. Solicit feedback.
4. Evaluate performance.

Define Competencies

Every member of the team has been selected to support the needs of the project. Individuals are recruited for their level of knowledge, skills, and attributes. Once the project has been scoped and planned, each member of the team should know what is expected of him or her upon joining. A one-page list of standards is often all that is needed to set expectations and clarify team member roles.

For the sake of example, let's say I am leading a project team responsible for implementing a new customer service system. I have identified and recruited team members. We have initiated and planned the project, clarified team goals, and identified supporting team behaviors. We have conducted a Rules of Engagement exercise. Now that the standards for both project and team success have been set, it is time to communicate expectations to my team so each individual team member knows what is expected of him or her and what defines success.

The Project Team Competency template (figure 4-3) allows the project team leader to identify and communicate what is expected of each team member assigned to the project. The tool not only establishes performance expectations but also acts as a guide to assess individual team member performance throughout the life cycle of the project.

My one-page project team competency template might look something like figure 4-4.

What It Is

The Team Competency Template instills accountability across team members and gives all team members the opportunity to maximize their skills, do the best work they are capable of, and continue to grow and learn while assigned to projects. The competencies reflect the knowledge, skills, and attributes needed to enable each project team member to achieve high performance while supporting the demands of each assigned project.

Why It's Useful

The Team Competency Template informs project team members of what is expected of them while on project assignment.

How It's Used

The template includes three levels of proficiency for each competency that has been identified as critical for the employee. The team leader informs the team member what is expected of him or her during the early team/project launch. At the end of the project, the project team leader completes the competency list by placing an "x" in the column that best represents the employee's overall proficiency level in each competency.

Figure 4-3 Project Team Competency Template

During the life of the project, it is important, as the team leader, to periodically revisit the list of expectations with each team member, to provide feedback, and to ensure expectations align with the evolution and continuation of the project. Unless each team member has a defined and confirmed set of expectations, how can she or he be held accountable?

It is the team leader's responsibility to assess the strengths and the weaknesses of each project team member and clearly and continually communicate them to team members. Don't allow the matrix environment

Competency proficiency level	Individual Contributor	Team Member
Industry knowledge	X	X
Organizational skills	X	X
Subject matter expertise	X	X
Treat each other with dignity and respect		
Exchange the needs and impacts of your own work with others		X
Actively seek and receive feedback for improvement		X
Make timely decisions and solve problems quickly		X
Analytical skills	X	

Figure 4-4 Example of Team Competency Template

to interfere with this process. When staff are allocated to a project team, the project manager should have full ability and authority to share performance feedback directly with project team members, regardless of direct or functional reporting relationships.

Team members who receive real feedback in real time have a real opportunity to improve. Imagine giving project team members the opportunity to improve their performance while serving the project needs versus their learning of improvement opportunities when it's too late—after the project ends. Too often project team members are informed of performance issue opportunities after the project ends and the team is disbursed; stale feedback limits performance improvement.

In many organizations, project managers are not given the "authority" to directly manage project team members; it is considered the functional manager's responsibility to fulfill this role. How can a functional manager effectively manage a staff member's performance if the staff member is spending all or most of his or her time on a project?

Project managers should be responsible for managing project team members' performance during the life of the project. In fact, the project manager should have this clearly stated as a required responsibility.

Interestingly, too few project managers have managerial responsibilities identified when clarifying their roles or job description. All project managers should have both the authority and the ability to exchange feedback for improvement to support their individual growth as real managers and the growth and development of team members while assigned to the project.

Set Expectations

Team accountability exists when all members of the group individually and collectively act to consequentially promote the timely delivery of the project's goal. Establishing and documenting expectations and communicating them to all members of the team support this objective. The one-page grid sets expectations and guides a conversation with each team member so each person knows how to act individually and collectively; it also sets performance standards.

Solicit Feedback

The competency grid not only sets expectations with individual team members early in the project life cycle, but it also acts as the gauge to evaluate performance when the project ends. Performance feedback is necessary throughout the project. It should not be saved until the project is completed. Performance feedback is successful when clear expectations are established early in the project launch and when solid feedback is solicited during project activities.

For example, if the project I described above has successfully closed, I can rely on my project team competency template to evaluate performance (figure 4-5).

Competency Proficiency Level (Place X in appropriate box below)					
	Individual Contributor	Team Member	Exceeds	Meets	Needs Improvement
Industry knowledge	X	X			
Organizational skills	X	X			
Subject matter expertise	X	X			
Treat each other with dignity and respect		X			
Exchange the needs and impacts of your own work with others		X			
Actively seek and receive feedback for improvement		X			
Make timely decisions and solve problems quickly	X	X			

Figure 4-5 Evaluating Performance Using Project Team Competency Template

Evaluate Performance

The key to a successful evaluation is to have clearly established definitions and standards associated with each level of performance. For example, the levels noted above may be defined as follows:

- *Exceeds expectations.* Performance was consistently and clearly above expected levels, and contributions were made in areas beyond the normal responsibilities of the position. Work was superior in quality, merit, and/or skill, and the project team member went beyond what one would normally expect.

- *Meets expectations.* Performance was at expected level in critical job areas, and the team member met and sometimes exceeded all objectives and expectations.

- *Needs improvement.* Significant additional and/or improved performance is required to bring performance to an acceptable level within a specified timeframe.

Finally, it is important to make the expectations real by defining the consequences of individual or team actions. All too often, team leaders shy away from taking real action when performance does not meet stated expectations. This occurs for a variety of reasons, ranging from the challenges of a matrix environment, where the project manager has little direct authority over team members, to the opposite extreme, where the project manager over-focuses on fielding complaints from project stakeholders but spends little time addressing individual or team accountability.

If teams are to be held accountable in a real and meaningful way, they must handle the results of their own actions together—as a team. This requires team members to be in regular contact with project stakeholders in order to get timely feedback. It also means establishing a team culture where the whole team is held accountable for the performance of each member.

In a true team-based culture, coaching and correcting individual performance problems is as much a team responsibility as a management responsibility. Team leaders can promote such a culture by regularly asking team members, "How are we doing as a team?" and/or "How am I performing as team leader?"

Organizations that are real about promoting teamwork and accountability tie compensation to performance. Organizations that tie rewards and compensation to team output allow teams to share in the financial success of the project, the team, and the organization. The culture of an organization is just as powerful as its systems in determining how much accountability people will accept.

Creating a culture of accountability means creating a climate in which staff can speak openly and admit to mistakes without fear; for many, the greatest challenge associated with this practice is the fear of being punished for their actions. Busting the cycle of blame starts with the way team members behave with each other. Teams can identify and agree on how they will be held accountable during the rules of engagement exercise.

The key to success is acting according to the Rules of Engagement (see chapter 3). Saying the words is a start; documenting them is better; and putting them into action is ideal. The value of addressing accountability during the rules of engagement exercise is that it allows you, as the team leader, to open the discussion for all team members, rather than you as the leader dictating what is expected. The magic is created when team members share best practices from previous experiences; once such practices are combined, you have a terrific platform to set expectations across the team as a whole.

Changing from a culture of blame to one of support always boils down to how each member behaves with the others. For team leaders, here are a few sound strategies to help foster a culture of shared accountability:

- Establish trust among team members. This means doing what you say and saying what you mean all the time. If we do not consistently follow through on our commitments to the team, we quickly become the weakest link.

- Openly admit to your own mistakes and accept the consequences for them.

- Be explicit about expectations. Talk openly and frequently about roles and responsibilities, performance expectations, deliverables and deadlines, and the implications of not communicating identified risks early.

- Balance your message of accountability with supportive actions that help teach and coach others to new levels of success.

Having a culture of accountability within your team ensures team members are doing their part "right" and are collectively supporting the overarching goal of the team. As the team becomes more cohesive and team members are held accountable in positive and principled ways, people will fulfill the expectations of the team, which ultimately supports organizational success. A team culture of collaboration and accountability can bring about exceptional results.

PART II

MAKING THE TEAM WORK

Once the project team has been launched, the challenge becomes making it work as a cohesive, productive unit. The keys to accomplishing this are addressed in the following chapters:

Chapter 5. Managing Team Conflict.   Conflict on teams is inevitable. Regardless of how high-performing your team might be, it will experience some type of conflict during its existence. If managed well, however, conflict does not need to be a negative and destructive experience.

Chapter 6. Making Effective Decisions.   Much of what project managers do is solve problems and make decisions. Project managers and project team members are often "under the gun"; they are required to deliver a project under very tight deadlines. Consequently, many project teams, when encountering a new problem or facing a decision, react with a decision that seemed to work before. This might work in the short term, but it's easy to get stuck in a circle of solving the same problem over and over again.

Chapter 7. Actively Sharing Information.   Regardless of team size or team type, team members who appreciate their needs and the impacts of their own work on others will be more inclined to act quickly and perform well together. Teams that draw up guidelines for how to make and refuse requests tend to be more successful than teams that do not.

Chapter 8. Holding Productive Meetings.   Today's competitive environment forces organizations to be nimble and efficient. More often than not, organizations believe they are being productive through the overuse of business meetings. We call meetings to inform, to decide, to analyze, and to assess. If not managed properly, meetings do not produce business results and are not an effective use of time. This is especially true when we manage virtual meetings.

CHAPTER 5

Managing Team Conflict

Any intelligent fool can make things bigger, more complex, and more violent. It takes a touch of genius—and a lot of courage—to move in the opposite direction.

—Albert Einstein

We are a very diverse society, and this is reflected in the workplace and in our teams. Differences in ideas, interests, values, culture, and perceptions between individuals or within groups make conflict inevitable in certain circumstances. Although conflict can often be a risk for a team, it can also lead to learning and growth; it can be a stimulus for new ideas and solutions that otherwise might not be identified. In fact, effectively managed conflict can produce a win-win situation for all involved.

THE ANATOMY OF CONFLICT

Many of us dislike conflict and prefer to avoid it rather than confront it. Understanding the anatomy of conflict and developing strategies for dealing with it allow us to address it head-on. If we don't learn how to deal with conflict, the danger is that when conflict arises, the situation will soon escalate into something destructive that causes long-term damage to relationships and teamwork.

In fact, unresolved conflict tends to escalate as each party attempts to defeat and destroy the other, each believing himself or herself to be "right." Teams must acknowledge that conflict will occur and agree to ways to address and resolve conflict as soon as possible, so all parties involved, directly and indirectly, can reestablish productivity.

Conflict is not necessarily the result of clashing personalities. In fact, personalities don't clash—behaviors do! Different people can work together for a long time without having conflict until their behaviors conflict. Differentiating personality from behavior makes conflict manageable.

Differences in opinion tend to cause conflict, as most people don't recognize that these differences can be positive. The ability to make use of differences in a healthy way often leads to learning opportunities, new discoveries, and innovative solutions. The key to success is how teams constructively manage differences and avoid negativity.

Establishing rules of engagement (discussed in chapter 3) allows team members to identify and agree to a set of behaviors and expectations as to how team members will act when dealing with conflict. For example, a group that agrees that passive-aggressive behavior or a condescending tone is not acceptable within the team structure is taking the first step to prevent such behaviors from occurring.

Understanding and appreciating different personalities among the group is important, but it is not necessarily a means of preventing conflict from occurring. Personality tests are very popular in business today. Many organizations invest significant time and resources in having staff participate in personality assessments, hoping the results will promote individual awareness, heighten sensitivity to diversity, enhance group interactions, and reduce conflict. The most popular personality type assessments available today include the Myers-Brigg Indicator, the DISC Assessment, and Don Lowry's Color Personality System.

The Myers-Briggs Type Indicator® (MBTI) helps people better understand themselves and how they work with others.[1] The DISC Assessment is a four-quadrant behavioral model based on the work of William Moulton Marston, PhD, to examine the behavior of individuals in their environment or within a specific situation. It focuses on the styles and preferences of such behavior.[2] Don Lowry's Color Personality System further simplifies the language used to discuss personality by using colors—blue, green, gold, and orange—as a way to easily recognize and understand personality differences.[3]

Personality profiling systems offer helpful insights. The results of personality indicators inform people about their own personality characteristics and enable them to become sensitive to others' results. This is great information to have when establishing or joining new teams.

Many project teams, however, do not have the luxury of indulging in such assessments; the project demands don't allow them to delve deeply into personality analytics. Today's project teams are often thrust together and expected to get the job done as quickly as possible. As a result, most project teams must share a common understanding:

- Everyone on the team is unique, with distinctive personalities and working styles.
- Teams must anticipate conflict.
- We should identify ways to mitigate discord with which everyone can live.

When teams acknowledge they will face conflict, find simple ways to deal with conflict, and move on, they are likely to take conflict in stride rather than being derailed by it. Conflict, when managed well, can lead to learning and growth for teams. It can be a stimulus for new ideas and solutions that otherwise might not be identified.

In the heat of conflict, it is common to "blow off steam." But steam can be a positive source of renewed energy. When used properly, steam can propel a train, so just think of what a little can do for a team! Effectively managed conflict can produce a win-win situation for everyone involved.

Teams must establish a conflict resolution process that is acceptable for everyone on the team. The rules of engagement exercise presented in chapter 3 prompts teams to discuss conflict, collect team members' views regarding conflict, and establish a process to resolve conflict when it occurs. The process should be simple and easy to follow, regardless of what type of conflict is experienced.

In most cases, a four-step process is all that is needed:

- Step 1: Individuals will try to resolve the conflict with each other.
- Step 2: If two individuals cannot resolve the conflict, the team leader will intervene.
- Step 3: If the team leader cannot facilitate resolution, an outside facilitator will mediate.
- Step 4: Once the conflict is resolved, other team members will be apprised of the outcome.

As simple as the four-step process might be, it is important that all team members understand and accept the process. The discussion instills a level of accountability for each team member regarding conflict management, it reinforces the concept that all members are individually responsible for resolving conflict and it solidifies the group's overall goal to resolve conflict quickly.

When faced with conflict, most of us prefer to avoid it rather than confront it. The danger with this strategy is that if we don't deal with conflict when it occurs, the situation can easily escalate into something destructive that causes long-term damage to relationships and teamwork.

Conflict between individuals that remains unresolved tends to escalate until each party attempts to defeat the other. Not only is this destructive to the individuals directly involved, but it can also infect their teammates as well. The key is to find the right time and way to deal with conflict.

When conflict arises during a team meeting, address the issues as soon as possible. If the conflict has nothing to do with the topic at hand, defer it to a later time. If the disagreement gets overheated, take a break and let everyone cool off.

THE ONE-DAY RULE

The one-day rule (see figure 5-1) is a great way to handle conflict and to address contention among teammates. It is an effective way to resolve unresolved discord in a timely manner, while also allowing you to regain composure before addressing the other party. It involves waiting exactly one day from the initial point of conflict. The one-day rule encourages you to address and resolve conflict within a day of the incident.

Consider this scenario:

Two team members have a direct disagreement during a team meeting. The two parties have different viewpoints and are unable to resolve their differences. There is a verbal confrontation, causing teammates to feel uncomfortable. The team members are derailed by the disagreement and find themselves challenged to get back on track. The atmosphere becomes thick and more competitive. The team leader finally suggests the issue be taken off-line for resolution.

In most cases, the two parties directly involved have lost clarity and focus on the real issue; in fact, the parties might have lost sight of the real issue altogether. After the meeting ends, one of the parties directly involved in the heated dispute approaches a few other teammates, wanting to gossip about the other person. Before anyone realizes it, the original issue becomes bigger and bigger; the conflict spreads among team members; and as more individuals lose sight of the original strife, it is likely the entire team will become less focused on the project's needs.

In this particular situation, the one-day rule could have reinforced the concept of resolving the conflict as soon as possible (within one day of the incident), preventing the conflict from growing as time lingered.

What It Is

The one-day rule supports quick resolution to one-on-one conflict and helps resolve discord by dealing with the disagreement directly and professionally.

Why It's Useful

The step-by-step process guides team members to resolve conflict quickly and efficiently. The process allows involved parties time to cool down from the initial conflict while also supporting the notion that the quicker the conflict is resolved, the faster the team can refocus on the work to be done.

How It Works

Under the one-day rule, all team members accept there will be conflict at some point during the team's tenure. Team members agree to address one-on-one conflict within one day of the initial clash.

Steps

1. Recognize you had some part in the situation and reflect upon your part.

2. Within one day of the disagreement, contact the person who has upset you and request a convenient time to talk.

3. Acknowledge the disagreement and express your desire to address it, resolve it, and move on.

4. Make a good-faith effort to understand, accept, and validate the other person's viewpoint.

5. Ask, "What do we need to do to put this behind us?" Agree to not hold a grudge or to use the incident to leverage any future disagreements.

6. If the conflict occurred in a team setting, inform team members of the resolution so as not to distract or impede the team's forward momentum.

Figure 5-1 One-Day Rule

7. Put the incident behind you and move on, focusing on the project needs.

Tips

- Listen keenly to each other and try to understand each others' position.

- Use face-to-face communication, if possible. Conversation over the telephone or by email should be used only when distance precludes a face-to-face meeting.

- Every team member involved in the conflict are equally accountable for attempting to resolve it, regardless of who initiated the dispute.

- Consider personal differences when using this process; some personality types feel extremely uncomfortable with direct confrontation.

- Adopt the one-day rule as the team's conflict resolution strategy during the Rules of Engagement discussion.

- Team members should remain focused on resolving the conflict by keeping the issue between them. They should not involve others for backup or opinion.

- If unable to reach a resolution, seek intervention from the team leader or an outside facilitator.

Figure 5-1 One-Day Rule (*Continued*)

Although dealing with conflict directly and immediately is a good course of action, there are times when avoidance or delay works better. For example, you might find yourself in the wrong place at the wrong time. Suppose your teammate did not like your behavior in the team meeting that just ended. You are confronted in the hallway, as you head back to your cubicle. Having a heated discussion in a public area might not be the best way to address the issues. The time and place might not be right; maybe you are not in the right mood to confront the conflict head-on. For a variety of reasons, you know your current state of mind will not work toward resolving the conflict. You need to avoid the issue until you can focus on it fully and calmly.

The one-day rule suggests you wait a while before you react or respond to a squabble. If you feel your blood rising, your pulse quickening, and your breath shortening, apply the one-day rule by saying, "Let me think about this. Can we talk about it tomorrow?" This response beats the finger you were about to point back in their direction.

When you force yourself to wait a day, you are able to take control of your thoughts. You can have the presence of mind to know what you are thinking, and you can avoid a behavior that you might regret later. You allow yourself time to cool off. A good night's sleep can dramatically change your perspective.

Waiting a day before reacting is particularly useful when communicating by email. Sometimes our fingers have a way of working before our brains think things through. Nothing is worse than regretting your actions immediately after clicking "Send" during a heated email exchange. In some circumstances, we need time to get back into our own heads to be at our best. When you take the time to cool off and calm down, you can validate the real issue at hand and address it with appropriate actions and response. Take 24 hours to ensure you act from your best.

Waiting a bit before you address discord enables you to accomplish two things: It allows you to calm down and it allows you to refocus on the real issue. Most conflict occurs when a problem cannot be solved or a decision cannot be made. Lack of problem-solving and decision-making skills often leads to unresolved issues, affecting the team's ability to return to accomplishing the work at hand. There is more on this in chapter 6.

Often, conflict arises during decision-making and problem-solving. The next chapter explores how to effectively make timely decisions and solve problems quickly.

Notes

1 The Meyers-Briggs Type Assessment® was first developed in 1943 by Catherine Cook Briggs and Isabel Briggs Meyers. For more information on this personality assessment tool, see the MBTI website at http://www. myersbriggs.org/my-mbti-personality-type/mbti-basics (accessed June 10, 2010).
2 DISC is a group of psychological inventories developed by John Geier and others and is based upon the 1928 work of psychologist William Moulton Marston and others. For more information about the DISC Assessment, go to its publisher's website at http://www.inscapepublishing.com (accessed June 10, 2010).
3 Carolyn Kalil, *Follow Your True Colors to the Work You Love* (Wilsonville, OR: BookPartners, Inc., 1998).

CHAPTER 6

Making Effective Decisions

For every problem there is an opportunity.

—Chinese Proverb

Decision-making comes more naturally to certain personalities. People who are less natural decisionmakers are often able to make quality assessments but need to be more decisive in acting on the assessments made. On teams, it is important to draw on the innate powers of everyone on the team to reach agreement and then act on it.

Problems are inevitable when managing projects. All projects, regardless of size, type, and duration, will experience problems during their life cycle.

There are many approaches to problem-solving, depending on the nature of the problem and the people involved in the problem. The more traditional, rational approach is typically used in business settings and on project teams. It includes four steps:

- Clarify the problem.
- Identify options.
- Make a decision.
- Implement the solution.

CLARIFY THE PROBLEM

Einstein said you cannot solve a problem until you define it. Defining the problem is often where people struggle. They react to what they think the problem is. Instead, seek to understand more about why you think there is a problem.

There are a number of questions you and your team can ask as you clarify the problem:

- What can you see that causes you to think there's a problem?
- Where are we now?
- How is it happening?
- When is it happening?
- Why is it happening?

This series of question helps members of the group confer with one another to verify the problem. It also provides an opportunity to prioritize the problem, especially when the problem is complex. If the problem seems overwhelming, break it down until you have descriptions and agreements of several related problems. Solving smaller, more manageable issues is often easier and quicker than handling one guerrilla-size issue.

IDENTIFY OPTIONS

Teams have the ability to speed up or bog down this phase of the process. Identifying options in a team setting is successful only when all members are actively involved. In a team setting, brainstorming works well because it collects as many new ideas as possible and then screens them to find the best idea.

Don't make the brainstorming process complicated. You can manage the process by asking the group one simple question: "What options do we have?" Then list all the ideas. It is important to not pass judgment on the ideas generated through the brainstorming process.

How you reach your preferred options can also be a simple process. Let's face it. Most project teams are under the gun to get the work done in a very short time. The more streamlined the process, the more likely teams will follow it and find success. To make a decision is to make a choice. To make the best decision, we need to know what options are available to us.

One method is to use the following preferred options tool (see figure 6-1) to help the team identify a short list of preferred options.

MAKE A DECISION

Before we talk about various decision-making models, we should understand the nature of decisions in relation to problem-solving. A variety of elements influence our decisions, including the number of options available, our past experiences, our beliefs and prejudices, our gut feelings, personal circumstances (i.e., how vested we are in the outcome), how quickly the decision has to be made, and other people's opinions.

Many decisions are not made purely on logic but include a complex blend of perception, thinking, and judgment. Sensation and intuition support the perception function; feeling, emotion and morality support our judgment; and thinking is derived by logic, analysis, and argument.

Intuition, according to Carl Jung, is perception using the subconscious. It helps us to see things from a different perspective, and it may help us to see deeper relationships, patterns, and potential. It should not be undervalued. The key to successful decision-making is to recognize the value of intuition and the importance of facts and logic.

Having too many options will often make the decision-making process less effective. The objective is to identify a short list of preferred options and quickly select the best one. You should also have a clear understanding of when the decision needs to be made; the amount of time available to make a decision can impact the inclusiveness of the decision-making process.

What It Is

The preferred options tool allows the team to identify and inventory options in order to make an effective decision.

Why It's Useful

When teams are faced with making decisions with limited data or within short timeframes, the pressure of it all can sometimes derail groups from making the best decision—or any decision. The preferred options tool keeps teams focused on possible solutions, enabling them to make the best decision at the right time.

How It Works

1. When facing a decision, start the process by declaring the due date for the decision. This is important so everyone on the team knows when the decision must be made.

2. Determine how the decision will be made and who will be involved in making it.

   - Is it a consensus decision?
   - Will information be solicited from the team, allowing the team leader to decide?
   - Will the team leader decide and simply inform others?
   - Will someone outside the team make the decision with or without input from the team and team leader?

3. List all possible options on the preferred options tool, including the pros and cons associated with each option.

4. Facilitate group discussion focusing on each identified option. As the discussion advances, options may iterate; be sure to capture all ideas and variations.

5. Make the decision, document the results, and communicate accordingly.

Figure 6-1 Preferred Options Tool

Preferred Options

Decision Needed:_____

Due Date:_____

Option #1:_____

Description:		
How could it work?		
Advantages:	Disadvantages:	This option can be improved by:

Option #2: _____

Description:		
How could it work?		
Advantages:	Disadvantages:	This option can be improved by:

Decision:_____

Agreed on:_____

Figure 6-1 Continued

If the timeframe is very short, one person or a subset of the team might need to make the decision. If this is the case, it is important for the decisionmaker to inform the rest of the team quickly. The amount of analysis done to determine the most appropriate solution should be in direct proportion to the degree of risk associated with the problem.

A multitude of decision-making models are available to teams today. Keeping the team focused on a short list of effective options will streamline the decision-making process. Four approaches can be employed by project managers when a decision needs to be made:

- *Tell.* The project manager makes a decision without the involvement of others. Those affected are simply told what the decision is, after it has been made.

- *Consult.* Those affected are consulted before a decision is made, and their ideas/concerns are listened to carefully. However, responsibility for the final decision still rests with the team leader.

- *Negotiate.* A decision is agreed upon by those affected. The team leader and the team members work together to build an understanding of the various parties' needs and feelings, and they try to find the best possible solution to the problem or situation.

- *Devolve.* The decision is left up to the team. Responsibility for the decision rests fully with the team, although the parameters are likely to be agreed on by the team leader in advance. In this scenario, decisions are typically made through consensus.

These approaches should be used as guides; each decision is unique and should be regarded as such. Each approach may also require the involvement of a higher authority to guide the decision-making process or to make the decision outright.

In some instances, the magnitude of the decision might require that the decision be made by someone outside the team itself. In such instances, someone outside the team makes the decision with or without input from the team and the team leader. The team as a whole should anticipate these needs in advance, so everyone clearly understands the chain of command in the decision-making process.

At a bare minimum, all teams should discuss decision-making models and understand what level of decision-making is available. Ideally, this conversation and understanding should occur in advance of any decision's being made, so everyone has a clear appreciation of what decisions can be made within the team confines versus what decisions require a higher authority.

For many project teams, it is often the project sponsor who is able to make decisions once a certain level is reached. Ideally, all key players in the decision-making process should be involved in the decision-making discussion so everyone has a clear expectation of roles, responsibilities, and relationships when decisions are required.

I recently had a discussion with a project manager and his project team. I asked, "Does everyone on the team understand what level of decision-making you have?" They all nodded their heads in unison, indicating *yes*. The project manager added, "Yes, it's our project sponsor." I followed up with another question: "Does the project sponsor know this?" A few members on the team looked at one another, confused. The silence among the teammates lingered for a few more seconds. Finally, the project manager replied, "No, I don't think we've actually had a direct discussion."

Never guess what level of decision-making authority you have. Know what you can decide, the level of decision authority you have, and to whom you should go when you need a decision from someone else. Imagine the amount of time you can save during the decision-making process when everyone on the team has this information *before* a decision needs to be made.

When time allows, it is helpful to take time to reflect on decisions recently made. How can you verify that the problem has been resolved if you don't consider a few key questions?

- Did we effectively resolve the issue?
- What changes should be made to avoid this type of problem in the future?
- What did we learn from this problem-solving?

Consider new knowledge, understanding and/or skills. Consider writing a brief note that highlights the success of the problem-solving effort and what you and your team learned as a result. This is a terrific addition to your lessons learned process when formally closing the project.

IMPLEMENT THE SOLUTION

Once the decision has been made, it must be acted upon. The decision-making process is often hard and stressful; not acting upon the decision once it's made is almost like making no decision at all, offering no value for involved project team members or the project itself. A good way to promote the importance of both making the decision and acting upon it is by documenting both the decision and the follow-up action at the same time.

Figure 6-2 offers an easy way to track both the decision and the action to support the decision.

Implementing solutions requires the same level of rigor and discipline as implementing the entire project. The project team should document a plan of action and follow it to ensure the decision or solution to the problem is carried out in a complete and timely manner. Solution implementation is typically task driven and should involve a sequence of activities. The plan of action should state what needs to be done, how much it will cost, when it needs to be done, and by whom. Solutions are successfully implemented when expectations are clearly set, timelines are closely monitored, and communications among team members is constant.

Decision Needed	Due Date	Decision Maker(s)	Action Steps	Comments

Figure 6-2 Decision-Action Tracking Chart

As teams adopt expected behaviors and embrace team dynamics, there are other ways to enhance team output. In the next chapter, we'll look at how important actively sharing information is to effective project team operations.

CHAPTER 7

Actively Sharing
Information

Is there anyone so wise as to learn by the experience of others?

—Francis Voltaire

There is a lot of dancing on teams. Some members dance to their own tune as individual contributors; other members dance in pairs—one leads, the other follows in a partnership of give and take. At other times, a group dance might occur, where everyone on the team is stepping to the same rhythm and beat.

Regardless of what type of dance occurs and when, all participants must learn how to give and take and be prepared to change their dance step to match the changing rhythm of the project. Team members, like dancers, are at their best when they are flexible, nimble, and light on their feet.

ASSESSING INDIVIDUAL BEHAVIORS

Just as dances vary, individual behaviors vary. People naturally tend toward aggressive, submissive, or assertive behavior. Team members who understand what triggers certain behaviors in a group setting and who can also predict how others will behave in certain situations are more likely than others to thrive in a team setting and know how to effectively rely on each other to get the job done.

Team members who tend toward predominantly *submissive* behavior are those who are meekly obedient. They often respond in a dutiful manner and are pliable. In other words, submissive people are likely to be very accommodating of others' needs but pay little attention to their own. When a submissive team member seeks something from someone else, the result is likely to be a lose/win situation. The submissive party considers the other party's rights, needs, and feelings but fails to give proper consideration to his or her own rights, needs, and feelings.

Aggressive behavior, on the other hand, is considered forceful and confrontational. It is likely to result in a win/lose situation. Aggressive team members demonstrate their own rights and consider their own needs and feelings, but they give little regard to the rights, needs, and feelings of others.

Often, people will tend toward aggressive or submissive behavior when faced with situations that are outside their comfort zone or when dealing with "difficult" people. Our choices about what behavior to adopt are often influenced by our previous experiences and our personal values and beliefs.

Yet, our behaviors are likely to change with every situation. A "hard" team leader, for example, might be a complete pushover with her children at home. Our behaviors are often influenced, in part, by those around us. At work, corporate culture plays a significant role in driving how we, and others, behave.

In one organization, an aggressive, macho culture may be prevalent, while in another a more facilitative, non-blame culture may be dominant. So, in one organization, the belligerent team leader who forces his or her opinions on others and fights his or her way to the top might be admired, whereas the accommodating, cooperative leader might be viewed as soft, with little authority. In another organization, the opposite could be true.

Each of us views the world from a slightly different perspective. Our different views, different beliefs, and different experiences influence our attitudes and our behaviors. Understanding others' perspectives can help us find a middle way through dialogue. Take the time to discuss differences up front to eliminate confusion later.

Successful team members are *assertive*. Assertive behavior is likely to result in a win/win situation. Acting in an assertive manner enables you to demonstrate your own rights and consider your own needs and feelings, while still respecting the other party's rights, needs, and feelings.

When making a request, consider the following:

- *Decide what you want.* Sometimes, it helps to think about what you don't want to clarify what you do want.
- *Get the other person's attention.* In doing this, consider the environment. If it's noisy or there are a lot of people around, the other person might be distracted. Think about whether now is a good time to get the person's full attention.
- *Consider body language.* How close are you to the other person? For example, is your body language intimidating or overly passive?
- *Make it personal.* Show you want the person's attention by using his or her name. Use "I" and "you" in your sentences. Avoid using "we"; it does not clearly state responsibilities.
- *Be concise.* Keep it simple. Don't waste the other person's time.
- *Empathize.* Before you request something of someone else, ask yourself, "Am I thinking about the impact of my request on others?"
- *Use an appropriate tone.* Avoid anger or sarcasm.
- *Listen for, and to, the other person's response.* You might be willing to change your request.

When someone makes a request of you, consider the following:

- Am I clear about what is being asked of me?
- Can I summarize what I've heard?
- Do I have a way of prioritizing this request against my current workload or competing priorities?

To build a clear understanding of needs and feelings in negotiation, you must have effective questioning and listening skills. Often people approach negotiation by adopting a position from which they will give ground only reluctantly and slowly. We tend to adopt this approach, for example, when we negotiate a major purchase such as a car or house. We often make an initial offer well below what we are really prepared to pay.

Too often, our ego becomes entangled with the position we adopt. Every time we give ground, our ego is knocked, which makes us less likely and less willing to do it again. Negotiations become a battle of wills, where the one who gives the most ground is viewed by himself or herself and others as the "loser." With this type of negotiation, the focus is on our own needs, with very little understanding of the other party's needs and feelings.

It is important to separate the people and personalities from the request. If you are the person making the request of someone else, be sure to describe your request. Include the rationale for the request, specifics about what you are asking for, and the date and time when it is needed. If you are the receiver of the request, make sure you understand the request by summarizing what you heard. Carefully consider your other responsibilities and priorities before you respond. Remember, it is always more helpful and ultimately more productive to honestly account for what is on your plate and realistically agree to only what you can actually do.

Sometimes, you have to say "no" to requests. Listen to your inner feelings. If you have a sinking feeling, it is likely you should say "no." In this instance, be direct. Make sure you use the word *no* so there are no misunderstandings. Be honest, and don't make up long-winded excuses or blame others. Finally, be fair. In other words, acknowledge the right of the other person to be upset. Be sure you emphasize that it is the request, not the person, that is being denied.

The art of negotiation includes talking together, repeating and revising the request until you achieve individual or team agreement. Be sure to close the negotiation with a clear phrase that specifically defines the outcome. Examples include:

- Yes, I will do that for you.
- No, I can't do that for you within the timeframe that you are requesting, but what I can do is….
- I partially agree. I can do [this] but not [that].

Regardless of team size or team type, team members who appreciate their own needs and the impacts of their work on others are more inclined to act quickly and perform well together. Teams that draw up some guidelines for how to make and refuse requests tend to be more successful than teams that do not.

ACTIVELY GIVING AND RECEIVING FEEDBACK

The term *feedback* comes from the rocket industry of the early 1950s, when scientists were in the process of perfecting the rockets that would eventually take Neil Armstrong to the moon in 1969. The term was used to describe the circular wireless communications between the telemetry instruments on the ground and those on the rocket. The exchange of information from onboard sensors to the ground station would instruct the rocket. When the instructions were carried out, the sensors on the rocket would report back to the ground station, creating a continuous feedback loop.

In two-way interpersonal communication, the exchange of feedback should work in a similar manner. Information from a sender is delivered to a receiver. The way in which feedback is delivered *and* received greatly influences the outcome. When done well, the exchange of feedback is continuous and impactful, resulting in perpetual improvement.

Stephen Covey, in *The Seven Habits of Highly Effective People*, notes, "Between stimulus and response is our greatest power—the freedom to choose."[1] It is this freedom of choice—the opportunity to think through how we should respond to any given situation—that can lift a communication event from disaster to growth.

In today's frenetic business environment, people need to know what's changing and what's staying the same, what's working and what's no longer working. Continual feedback supports that need.

Feedback is an important part of the communication process. Without it, we don't know when we've done something well or could perhaps improve on something. Many people find it much easier to give feedback when it is positive than when it is negative. However, people need to give and receive both on a regular basis. Doing so helps us become aware of ourselves, to realize the consequences of our actions, and to change or modify our behavior.

Positive feedback reinforces the development of the recipient and builds confidence. How do we know if we are doing a good job if no one tells us? Effective feedback can create a continuous cycle of improvement in confidence and ability. Positive feedback reinforces the standards we are expected to meet and shows that our performance and behavior are cared about and noticed. Positive reinforcement lets us know how we are doing and that our performance is headed in the right direction.

Negative feedback is equally important and helpful. Providing negative feedback helps the recipient who is a bit "off track" to refocus. Can you think of a time where, in retrospect, you were grateful that someone had given you negative feedback? It builds commitment and involvement among team members and can help identify training and development needs.

Constructive feedback can be positive or negative. It is related to a task or action that was well done or one that needs improvement. It is information-specific, focused on a specific issue, and direct in delivery. Constructive feedback does not include a "right or wrong" opinion; it is based on observation and is objective. When delivered properly, it encourages discussion and dialogue.

Praise or criticism, on the other hand, is a personal judgment about performance. It is usually based on general or vague information or on opinions and feelings, and it typically focuses on the person, not the behavior. Delivering praise or criticism does not promote discussion or dialogue between the giver and receiver.

Giving and receiving feedback is a shared responsibility across the team as a whole. In other words, the team leader should not be the only person responsible for providing feedback to others. Although the team leader is the primary person overseeing the project and must ensure all team members are contributing to the needs of the project, all members of the team are also responsible for how they interact with one another.

The skills of giving feedback and receiving feedback can be learned and, once practiced, can be extremely useful. Practice makes better; the more often feedback is shared, the more comfortable people become with both giving and receiving information. The only way for people to get better at what they do is for people they work for, and with, to provide candid, timely feedback sessions.

Ideally, all feedback exchanges should be conducted face-to-face. With more and more business conducted virtually, we often have less information than we need to understand where someone is coming from. Be sure to ask clarifying questions to get a full understanding of what is being described. This is particularly important when feedback is exchanged using email or voicemail. The lack of visible body language requires keener listening skills and the use of explicit, descriptive language.

Giving Feedback

Giving feedback is tough, but if the feedback is constructive, you will not only get the message across but also build a more cohesive and capable team. The ideal team culture includes all team members having equal comfort in giving and receiving feedback on a continual basis. Feedback that is limited to the annual performance review is less than ideal and is not very effective.

There are four aspects to providing constructive feedback:

- Content: What you say
- Manner: How you say it
- Timing: When you say it
- Frequency: How often you provide feedback.

What you say has lasting impact. It is important to provide specifics of what occurred (including examples of what you observed using verifiable facts). Feedback is not effective if it can't be supported by evidence, and firsthand evidence is better than that provided by others or through hearsay.

How you say it validates the information. When delivering feedback, don't say "We don't think…." Deliver your own feedback, using the word *I*. Be direct, and don't beat around the bush.

When someone is brave enough to ask for feedback, honor his or her request by being brief, concise, and factual in how you respond. Avoid "need to" phrases, which imply something didn't go well or is being judged. Be sincere. Avoid giving mixed messages, which are often called "yes…but" messages. For example, "Mary, you've worked hard on this task, but…." What follows is something Mary is not doing well, and that is the real point of the feedback. The attempt to sugar-coat is negated, and the sincerity of the message is diluted. Not only does the word "but" create contradictions in message, but it can also imply weakness in the person giving the feedback.

When giving positive feedback, express your appreciation together with specifics; this provides more value to your feedback than appreciation alone. For example, "Great job!" is appreciation on its own, as opposed to, "Jim, we were behind schedule last week and I noticed that without having to be asked, you pitched in and helped John get the project back on schedule. Thank you so much for helping out. Your initiative is really valuable to the team and to the project." In this example, the appreciation comes at the end, after the content is provided. It becomes real and sincere.

When providing negative feedback, recognize your tone of delivery. Tones of anger, disappointment, and sarcasm color the message, and then the message tends to be lost. State your observations, not your interpretations. Observations are what you see happening; interpretations are your analysis or opinions about what you going on. For example, "You've been moody today" is interpretive. "Today, I noticed that you were very quiet in our meeting, which has me concerned," is an observation, followed by authentic caring.

The goal of providing constructive feedback is to get the recipient to think about other approaches he or she might use, or to change a behavior. Use appropriate questions to engage the person and make feedback a two-way process. This is especially important when giving negative feedback. Some particularly useful questions include: "How do you feel it went?" "What would you do differently the next time?" "What other approaches could you have used?" These are all open-ended questions that encourage recipients to review their own performance and identify ways to improve or adjust it.

Normally, constructive feedback is most effective when it is provided as soon as possible—when the behavior or performance is still fresh in everyone's mind. There are, however, some instances in which providing negative feedback is better after a little time as passed.

Similar to how the One-Day Rule works, there is a fine line between being too quick and being too late in your response. Perhaps you need to cool off and get your thoughts in order, or allow the other party to cool off or think about his actions, before engaging in a discussion.

The Center for Creative Leadership (CCL) has a three-step process for effective feedback called the Situation-Behavior-Impact (SBI) model.[2] As the CCL states, "SBI provides a structure that helps keep your feedback focused and relevant, and increases the likelihood it will be received in a clear, non-defensive manner by the recipient." Here's how the approach works:

1. Describe the feedback in terms of the situation—yesterday at coffee, for instance. This helps the recipient connect and recall the time and place of his actions.
2. Describe the behavior—what was said or done. It helps the recipient to acknowledge the behavior.
3. Describe the impact the behavior had on you. Describing how it made you feel removes judgment and helps the recipient feel informed rather than attacked.

By following the SBI approach, you can package your feedback in a manner that shows respect and allows the recipient time to process it and understand the areas for improvement.

When giving feedback, be specific rather than general. The more concrete the feedback, the more useful it will be for the person receiving it. When you focus on specific behaviors or events, you are able to provide real examples rather than make general statements. Avoid generalizations such as "always," "never," "this," or "that."

Be descriptive rather than evaluative. Focus on the memo, the presentation, the accuracy of the report, etc. rather than how good or bad you perceive it to be. For example, rather than saying, "Janet, at times you were vague in your presentation..." tell Janet exactly where she was vague and how it affected her presentation.

Being specific requires that you be prepared. Put time and thought into what you are going to say and how you will deliver the message. Include as many details as you can. When citing an example, describe what the person did or said and how he or she did or said it. Be sure to describe the event, but don't judge it. If you are providing feedback around an emotionally charged event, take time to think it through. This is another example where the one-day rule applies.

Providing feedback is intended to be of value for the other person. It is a way to let people know how effective they are in what they are doing, or how they can improve their effectiveness. It provides a way for people to learn how to improve their behaviors and performance to become more successful.

Always lead with a positive item to show that you are aware of and recognize their contributions. Then deliver the constructive feedback in a thoughtful and planned manner so it is presented to support, not attack, the recipient. Presenting feedback in a judgmental, disrespectful, or attacking manner defeats the original intent of the feedback; the session is not intended to react to poor performance but rather to support improvements in performance.

When delivering feedback, make it have the impact it deserves by the manner and approach you use. Effective feedback should always focus on a specific behavior, not on the person or his or her intentions. Successful feedback describes actions or behavior that a person can do something about.

After the recipient accepts the feedback, the next step is to provide recommendations for improvement. Providing specific examples gives the recipient a starting point to begin improvement.

Soliciting and Receiving Feedback

Soliciting feedback does not need to be complex; in fact, the simpler, the better. People are busy with their own work and daily stresses, so asking them to take the time to provide feedback on their coworkers often takes some cajoling. One incentive is to appeal to people's self-interest: If you want feedback on yourself, be willing to provide it to others.

The feedback tool can be a simple questionnaire regarding staff adherence to the TEAM behaviors. Figure 7-1 provides an example.

What It Is

The TEAM behaviors feedback form is used to solicit feedback from team members about one's adherence to the expected behaviors.

Why It's Useful

People are more likely to correct their behavioral performance when they are informed of behavioral issues. This is particularly true on teams, where one team member's poor performance can derail an entire group. The tool promotes a team environment where team members become comfortable exchanging feedback for improvement as a routine practice.

How to Use It

Teams exchange the feedback form according to the team's schedule for exchanging feedback. The results can be shared individually or across the team, whichever is most comfortable for the team as a whole. The rating scale is 1–5:

0 – Unknown
1 – Strongly Disagree
2 – Disagree
3 – Neither Disagree nor Agree
4 – Agree
5 – Strongly Agree

To promote a rich exchange of actionable feedback, both the 1–5 rating scale and the comments section should be employed.

Figure 7-1 TEAM Behaviors Feedback Form

TEAM Behaviors Feedback Form

Staff Name_____

Date_____

Based on your observation of this employee, use the scale below to rate the use of each TEAM behavior and provide specific behavioral examples:

Rating Scale – Models the Use of TEAM behaviors

0 – Unknown

1 – Strongly Disagree

2 – Disagree

3 – Neither Disagree nor Agree

4 – Agree

5 – Strongly Agree

TEAM Behavior	0	1	2	3	4	5
Treat others with dignity and respect Comments / Examples of behavior:						
Exchange the needs and impacts of your own work with others Comments / Examples of behavior:						
Actively seek and receive feedback for improvement Comments / Examples of behavior:						
Make timely decisions and solve problems quickly Comments / Examples of behavior:						

Figure 7-1 TEAM Behaviors Feedback Form (*Continued*)

The information received through the survey process must be collected from a variety of people who are familiar with the person's performance and behaviors. It is important to solicit feedback from peers, colleagues, subordinates, customers, supervisors, and anyone else who has considerable interaction with the person throughout the performance period.

Once the feedback is received, it should be shared with the person, including all comments offered by participants. In fact, the comments received are always more valuable than the actual scores; they give specific information and might provide opportunities for technical or behavioral improvement.

Ideally, feedback must occur every day, not a few times a year. Team leaders can promote a culture of open communication by initially scheduling feedback sessions between team members on a regular basis. A mid-project check is highly encouraged. Monthly sessions are better, weekly is terrific, and daily is ideal. Scheduled feedback sessions promote the exchange of actionable information, enabling team members to give and receive constructive feedback in real time. Regularly scheduled sessions also enable team members to develop communication techniques in support of successful feedback exchange.

Another good practice to support timely exchange of feedback is to conduct a formal performance review at the close of a project. Collecting feedback within 30 days of project closure allows project teams to evaluate one another in real time, rather than waiting until the end of the calendar year. This provides project-related feedback while the experience is still fresh.

Evaluating project team members on both project delivery and TEAM behaviors provides a global view of a team member's technical and behavioral performance before he or she is assigned to the next project. The goal is to give staff the opportunity to take the feedback to heart before their next project experience, so areas identified for improvement may be addressed before their next project or team assignment.

Figure 7-2 is a simple form for collecting feedback on a project manager's performance after project closure.

What It Is

The project manager performance feedback tool is an easy way to solicit performance feedback on a project manager's performance.

Why It's Useful

The project manager is best equipped to act on performance issues when feedback is received in an honest and timely fashion. Ideally, performance feedback should be shared with a project manager within 30 days of project closure; this allows the project manager to act on the feedback received before his or her next project assignment.

How to Use It

Once the project closes, the project manager's functional manager sends the feedback tool to project team members, project stakeholders, and anyone else who was directly associated with the project activities and/or project results and is capable of providing performance feedback.

The functional manager collects and analyzes the feedback received and informs the project manager of the feedback, along with suggested tactics on how to improve in the areas noted as needing improvement. The feedback results allow for a rich discussion between the functional manager and the project manager, so the project manager is well equipped with real-time feedback information that is actionable.

Project Manager Performance Feedback Tool

To: <functional manager of a project manager>

From: <project team member>

Date: <place date here>

Re: **Performance Appraisal Input for <project manager's name>**

Figure 7-2 Project Manager Performance Feedback Tool

1) PM's understanding of project objective and ability to define goals for project team

Very Satisfied	Satisfied	Moderately Satisfied	Dissatisfied	Very Dissatisfied	Not Applicable
○	○	○	○	○	○

2) PM's facilitation and management of team meetings

Very Satisfied	Satisfied	Moderately Satisfied	Dissatisfied	Very Dissatisfied	Not Applicable
○	○	○	○	○	○

3) PM's ability to effectively lead a team

Very Satisfied	Satisfied	Moderately Satisfied	Dissatisfied	Very Dissatisfied	Not Applicable
○	○	○	○	○	○

4) PM's communication skills with various levels of staff ranging from entry-level to senior management

Very Satisfied	Satisfied	Moderately Satisfied	Dissatisfied	Very Dissatisfied	Not Applicable
○	○	○	○	○	○

5) PM's display of effective planning, tracking, and control

Very Satisfied	Satisfied	Moderately Satisfied	Dissatisfied	Very Dissatisfied	Not Applicable
○	○	○	○	○	○

6) PM's ability to manage risks, assumptions, issues, and decisions

Very Satisfied	Satisfied	Moderately Satisfied	Dissatisfied	Very Dissatisfied	Not Applicable
○	○	○	○	○	○

7) PM's ability to ensure deadlines and deliverables were met

Very Satisfied	Satisfied	Moderately Satisfied	Dissatisfied	Very Dissatisfied	Not Applicable
○	○	○	○	○	○

Expected Behaviors for Team Performance

Based on your observation of this employee, provide specific behavioral examples of the use of expected behaviors:

1. Treat others with respect and dignity

Comments/Examples of Behavior:

Figure 7-2 Project Manager Performance Feedback Tool (*Continued*)

2. **Appreciate the needs and impacts of own work on others**
   Comments / Examples of Behavior:

3. **Solve problems and make timely decisions**
   Comments / Examples of Behavior:

4. **Actively seek and receive feedback for improvement**
   Comments / Examples of Behavior:

   Other comments:

Figure 7-2 Project Manager Performance Feedback Tool (*Continued*)

Figure 7-3 provides a version that can be used for project team members.

Asking for feedback is the most difficult task in the feedback process. How you ask for feedback can affect the way you receive it. A great way to promote feedback exchange is for team members to incorporate simple questions into their routine dialogue with other team members; for example:

- How did I do delivering the presentation yesterday?
- Am I giving you what you need, when you need it, so the project delivers on time and on budget?

What It Is

The Project Team Member Performance Feedback Tool is an easy way to solicit performance feedback on a project team member's performance.

Why It's Useful

Project team members are best equipped to act on performance issues when feedback is received in an honest and timely fashion. Ideally, performance feedback should be shared with project team members within 30 days of project closure. This allows the project team member to act on the feedback received before his or her next project assignment.

How to Use It

Once the project closes, the project team member's functional manager sends the feedback tool to the project manager, other project team members, and anyone else who was directly associated with the project activities and/or project results and who is capable of providing performance feedback.

The functional manager collects and analyzes the feedback received and informs the project team member of the feedback, along with suggested tactics on how to improve in the areas noted as needing improvement. The feedback results allow for a rich discussion between the functional manager and the project team member, so the project manager is well equipped with real-time feedback information that is actionable.

Project Team Member Performance Feedback Tool

To: <functional manager of a project team member>
From: <project manager>
Re: **Performance Appraisal Input for <team member's name>**

Figure 7-3 Project Team Member Performance Feedback Tool

1. Areas of strength related to work as a team member on the project:

2. Areas where this team member is strong and could further enhance the strength or talent:

3. Areas where this team member has opportunity for development:

4. **Expected Behaviors**

   Based on your observation of this employee, provide specific behavioral examples of the use of Expected Behaviors:

   Treat others with dignity and respect

   Comments/Examples of Behavior:

   Appreciate the needs and impacts of own work on others

   Comments/Examples of Behavior:

   Solve problems and make timely decisions

   Comments/Examples of Behavior:

   Actively seek and receive feedback for improvement

   Comments/Examples of Behavior:

   Other comments:

Figure 7-3 Project Team Member Performance Feedback Tool (*Continued*)

- Where and when did [the specific behavior] occur?
- What are the observable actions that need to be changed or improved?
- I would like to improve my communication skills. Specifically, I'd like to make my points clearly and not wander off subject. Can you observe me and then speak with me afterwards about how I did?
- Do you have any suggestions for improvement?
- What do you view as my greatest strengths and assets to the team and this project?

When receiving feedback, consider the following:
- Although you might want to defend or explain your behavior by sharing your intentions, instead, listen intently to the behavior change that the person is suggesting.
- Ask clarifying questions: "What did you see?" "What was the impact on you?" "What did you think I was intending?"
- State your intention as you understand it. Ask and listen for the behavioral change that the person providing feedback is suggesting. Check to ensure your understanding.

If you are the recipient of feedback, listen intently. Do not become defensive or rationalize your behavior. Once you respond with a "no," "but," or "however," you have stopped receiving feedback. You cannot effectively listen while you are strategizing your defense. Do not interrupt the other person. You asked for the feedback; now listen to it.

CREATING A TEAM CULTURE CONDUCIVE TO SHARING INFORMATION

Organizations that make the management of group dynamics—and group project work—a major piece of their corporate culture reinforce both the awareness of and accountability for expected team behaviors through formal performance management activities. During the annual performance cycle, everyone is rated by their peers, supervisors, and teammates on each of the Expected Behaviors. It is a great way to build staff members' awareness of their behaviors and identify areas of strength and weakness for each behavior.

Projects include many interdependent tasks. Team members responsible for task completion must be aware of the interdependent relationships and appreciate that their individual performance affects the performance of other team members and their universal performance affects the success or failure of the project.

A good time to instill a team culture of open feedback is during the Rules of Engagement exercise. Typically, the conversation occurs while addressing the "Accountability" or "Operating Agreements" sections of the exercise. Not only is this a good time to introduce the concept of giving and receiving feedback, but it might also be a good time to identify best practices or simple techniques to support the behavior during team discussion. A simple statement, such as "We will all give and receive feedback on a regular basis," is enough to set the expectation and encourage frequent practice.

A team culture that includes the exchange of feedback can be built only when team members have a firm understanding of the characteristics of and differences between constructive feedback, praise, and criticism.

Giving and receiving feedback must be a two-way street. This isn't about team leaders informing team members of their shortcomings; it's about having an open dialogue to drive change in behaviors to promote ongoing development and success across team membership. To be successful, individuals must ExChange information. The ExChange formula looks like this:

$$\text{ExChange} = \text{Explicit} + \text{Change}$$

The intent of giving and receiving feedback is to engage in an exchange of explicit information that will prompt a change in behavior to improve performance.

Giving and receiving feedback can be scary, but the practice yields great rewards. I keep a small sticky note with three simple questions on my desk to remind me it's all about the feedback:

- How many times have you asked for feedback today?
- In the last week?
- In the last month?

Be brave. Ask for feedback. Be courageous and act on it. With continued practice, you will find seeking and receiving feedback easier to do with rewarding results.

Teams that operate in an open, honest environment, with trusting relationships, are more likely to produce better results than those that do not. In fact, all interactions among team members are more likely to produce efficient results when the group functions well.

Despite a trusting environment, however, team meetings often produce difficult challenges for most groups. We'll explore ways to hold productive, efficient meetings in the next chapter.

Notes

1 Stephen R. Covey, *The Seven Habits of Highly Effective People: Restoring the Character Ethic* (New York: Simon & Shuster, 1989).
2 The Center for Creative Leadership (CCL) is an international nonprofit educational institution whose mission is to advance the understanding, practice, and development of leadership for the benefit of society worldwide. For more information about the CCL or the SBI model, visit the CCL website at http://www.ccl.org/leadership/index.aspx (June 10, 2010).

CHAPTER 8

Holding Productive Meetings

Death by meetings. A slow and painful demise.

—Unknown

TEAM MEETING SCENARIOS

The Leadership Group

Wednesdays

8:00 am–10:00 am

The Leadership Group is a collection of 20 senior executives who meet every Wednesday morning to discuss corporate strategy, review operational performance, and track the progress of priority projects. The CEO is the facilitator and always starts the meeting on time. Most participants arrive before the meeting begins because the CEO always calls out late arrivers in a light, yet condescending, manner.

Without fail, Dan, the senior vice president of marketing, receives a call on his cell phone during the first half of the meeting. Dan's wife, Maria, is making her daily call to Dan to chat about miscellaneous activities at home. We can't help but listen. One week, we learn Dan and Maria are renovating their kitchen. On another occasion, we hear about their daughter's acceptance to college. Some weeks, Dan cuts Maria off too early in the call for us to know what the daily update is about; he glances around the room, lowers his voice, and declares, "I'm in a meeting. I'll have to call you back."

None of the calls between Dan and Maria last very long—two or three minutes at most. But regardless how brief the exchange, it disrupts the meeting. The entire team's focus has been interrupted; we have been taken off agenda. The CEO never addresses the weekly call. It continues to occur week after week. Eventually members of the team start placing bets before each meeting, predicting the time when Dan's phone will ring.

***

Mid-level Manager Meeting
Large Pharmaceutical Company
Thursdays
1:00 pm–3:00 pm

Twelve directors and four vice presidents meet each week to discuss project activities across their functional units. Most of the participants enter the meeting room armed with Blackberries and cell phones. It is common for participants to regularly read emails and accept phone calls throughout the two-hour meeting. The level of distraction becomes so significant that the group agrees to implement a new rule: All team members must surrender their electronic devices into a basket upon entering the room. Unfortunately, some people forget to shut off their devices before placing them in the basket. Buzzes, vibrations, and rings periodically emit from the communal basket, causing business to pause while members identify and then silence their disruptive devices. I wonder—how long does it take for the managers to claim their personal equipment when the meeting is over?

***

"CRM Project" Project Team Meeting
(10–14 members at any given meeting)
Tuesdays
10:00 am–11:00 am

The team meets weekly to discuss project status and to mitigate any risks that might impede project success. Approximately half of the team participate from remote locations; they conference-call into the meeting. I am invited to sit in today to observe the team dynamics of the group because the project manager believes the team is not functioning well. Participant attendance is spotty, and the project is running two months behind schedule. When the meeting begins, a number of key participants are noticeably absent. Members seldom notify the project manager in advance when they are unable to attend the meeting, and they never assign a delegate to attend in their place. Approximately 20 minutes into the meeting, a dog can be heard barking in the background through the spider phone. The dog continues to bark off and on throughout the meeting, making it difficult to hear everyone and to focus on the issues.

***

Joint Project Meeting
First and Third Thursday of Every Month
8:00 am–9:00 am

Two project teams support portions of the Member Enrollment Program, a highly visible and important initiative on the list of corporate priorities. The teams operate from two different campuses, with limited interaction between them. In the past three months, mistakes have been made, resulting in missed deliverables. Neither group wants to take accountability for the issues; there is a lot of finger pointing between units. As a result, biweekly meetings are scheduled so the teams can spend time together and discuss ways to improve their interdependent relationships.

A few minutes into their second meeting, a young women sitting toward the back of the conference room leans down, pulls a knitting needle out of her bag, and begins to knit. I find myself mesmerized by her activity. "What is she knitting?" I wonder. "Why is her knitting needle round?" Before I know it, I am no longer part of the team; I am mentally knitting along with her.

***

Project Review Meeting
Core Team Members, Project Sponsor, Project Customer
1:00 pm–3:00 pm

A project, preparing to transition from the planning phase to implementation, is under review. The PMO requires that all projects be reviewed at this point to ensure project planning is comprehensive and complete before the project is allowed to advance to implementation. The project manager gives a PowerPoint presentation involving a great deal of audience interaction and a lot of detailed analysis. He engages his audience. He poses questions, makes good eye contact, and answers questions in a thoughtful and comprehensive fashion.

The project sponsor sits at the back of the room, discreetly holding her Blackberry just under the edge of the table so no one can easily see her sending emails. Not once does the sponsor look up; it is obvious she is the only person in the room not paying attention.

Toward the end of the meeting, she sets her Blackberry aside, looks at the project manager, and says, "I'm not quite sure I completely understand where you and your team are coming from with this plan. Can we circle back and discuss this next week—same group, same time?"

What began as a useful meeting has quickly turned into a total waste of time. Nothing is worse than having to attend a follow-up meeting because an attendee at the original meeting wasn't paying attention.

***

Project Management Office
Staff Meeting
Tuesdays
1:00 pm–2:00 pm

The PMO staff meets weekly to review departmental activities, discuss the project portfolio, and assess global resource requirements. The group consists of five project managers and the director of the department. At this meeting, the group needs to design a new process to support new project requests to the project portfolio. Jim, a senior project consultant on the team, leads the discussion. As he walks the group through his proposal, there are questions from the team. A few people need additional details to fully understand Jim's recommendation. A few other members don't agree with the proposal and make suggestions on how to improve it.

Jim becomes visibly upset throughout the question-and-answer segment. He becomes defensive in both his answers and his body language. As the meeting progresses, Jim realizes the group is not comfortable with his proposal as designed. He looks at his teammates in disgust, gathers his belongings, and storms out of the meeting. His teammates look at each other in disbelief.

***

Do these team meeting scenarios sound familiar?

All teams should have standard meeting management practices to ensure productive results. Holding meetings that are effective, efficient, and engaging also encourages participants to attend meetings regularly—a must-have for successful meeting results. Almost all meetings have five phases:

- Before the meeting
- During the meeting
- Ending the meeting
- Assessing the meeting
- After the meeting.

Project teams can improve their meetings by applying some simple steps in support of each phase.

BEFORE THE MEETING

"What are we doing here?" How many times have you asked yourself that question while sitting through a meeting that had no direction?

When planning a meeting, you must know the purpose of the event. Understanding the purpose of the meeting helps you organize it properly. Ask the question, "What?" What, specifically, do you want to accomplish?

On the most basic level, meetings usually have one of two purposes: discussions (to get information) and briefings (to give information). Discussions rely on participant interaction. Participants share their ideas and opinions, contribute information, and possibly make decisions. Examples include staff meetings, creative meetings (brainstorming), and problem-solving meetings. Briefings, on the other hand, require little group interaction. Typically, one or more speakers provide information to a group of listeners. Examples include training sessions, sales presentations, and news conferences. If you know exactly what you want to accomplish going into the meeting, you are more apt to correctly define the type of meeting you need.

Meeting management does not need to be complicated to work. You can make your meetings stand APART from all others by following this advice:

- *Aim.* Before you arrange or schedule a meeting, make sure you understand its purpose. What is the meeting expected to achieve? What are its goals?
- *Preparation.* Now that you know what you want to achieve, what preparation is necessary? What will the agenda look like? What materials should be included with the agenda? What do you need to consider when choosing the setting or location for the meeting?
- *Audience.* Whom should you invite? What happens if you need someone's expertise for part of the meeting? What key roles do you need to fill within a meeting?
- *Results.* What needs to happen to ensure the meeting produces effective results? How will you track decisions, document action items, and manage due dates?

- *Time.* Do all agenda items have appropriate times assigned to them? How will you manage late arrivals to the meeting? What happens if topics arise that aren't on the agenda but are, nonetheless, important? How will the meeting end?

Take some extra time to think about why you are hosting a meeting and take extra effort to plan the meeting well. There is no point in scheduling a meeting if success is unlikely. Ask yourself the following questions when contemplating the need for a meeting:

- Do I have enough time to prepare for the meeting?
- Do other participants have the time to prepare themselves?
- Are all the necessary participants available and willing to attend?

If you can't answer "Yes" to all three questions, a meeting will likely be a waste of time.

Preparing for a meeting takes time and thought. It is not unusual to spend as much time planning a meeting as running a meeting. Preparation begins with asking these questions:

- What outcomes do we want to achieve?
- To achieve the desired outcomes, what must we do during the meeting?
- How much time will each item realistically require?
- What should I send to participants in advance?
- What information should we have available at the meeting?
- What's the best way to set up the space?
- What equipment will make the meeting run more smoothly?

Consider the "Input – Process – Output" model when planning your meeting. The IPO model allows you to plan your meeting by beginning at the end and working backwards. It involves three steps:

1. *Determine the Output.* What do you want to achieve? What is the purpose or goal of the meeting?

2. *Determine the Process.* What method(s) will you use to achieve the desired result or outcome?

3. *Determine the Input.* What materials (documents, visuals, etc.) will be required to complete the process and produce the output?

An easy and effective way to use the IPO process is to chart the three categories (output, process, and input) on a white board or easel. Using sticky notes, write down all the items that come to mind for each category. This will help you identify all the components required for a successful meeting. Once you have exhausted all possible items for each category, eliminate duplicates and tack each item under its corresponding category.

Sticky notes work particularly well because you can easily rearrange the items as you think through the process and sequence agenda items. Although the process of completing sticky notes may seem cumbersome to some, remember that having a visual list of items under each category forces you to holistically plan the entire meeting from start to finish. The act of writing down each item often prompts you to think about additional critical elements that otherwise might be missed.

Do not underestimate the power of visual thinking. After you have gained experience using the IPO process, you will become more familiar with the thought process, reducing the need for visual guidance. The IPO process is especially effective when planning a meeting with multiple parties. It is a terrific way to brainstorm all possibilities to support meeting success.

Once you have completed the IPO process, you can continue to plan your meeting by asking "Who?" Who should be invited? Invite only the people who need to be there. People will not be insulted if they are not invited to a meeting these days; most people have too many meetings to attend and are thrilled if not invited to a meeting that does not require their direct involvement or authority. A good rule of thumb is to always invite decisionmakers; often, non-decisionmakers can simply be informed after the fact.

Once you have your list of invitees, determine whether they all need to attend the meeting for the entire time. For example, can a subset of participants be invited only when a specific agenda item is being addressed? A well-crafted and well-managed agenda can almost always support this method.

The next question is "When?" When should the meeting be scheduled? The timing of your meeting is contingent upon two factors. First, be sure to allow enough time to prepare for the meeting. If, for example, the agenda includes additional materials requiring prework, be sure to give yourself enough time to prepare all the necessary materials and allow enough time for participants to do whatever they need to do with the materials before attending the meeting. Second, schedule the meeting on a date when all necessary participants are available. There is no point in scheduling the meeting according to your schedule if no one else can attend.

The fourth question is "Where?" Where should the meeting be held? Make the location convenient for participants, if possible. Pick a neutral spot, especially if you are trying to resolve conflicts or solve a problem. Identify a meeting room that will be conducive to a productive meeting. Consider the following questions to find the "right" location:

- Do you have adequate seating?
- Can the seats and tables be arranged the way you want them?
- Do you have appropriate equipment, technology, and services?
- Do you need backup support?

It is helpful to create a standard list of items typically required to support meetings to ensure you have what you need when you need it. Finally, if you are using technology or equipment of any kind, be sure you know how to operate all the devices and know who to call if you need additional support or assistance.

The last question is "How?" How long should the meeting last? If you have followed the IPO process, the answer to the last question should be easy.

In summary, meeting preparation requires four simple steps:

1. *Create a goal statement and distribute the goal with the meeting agenda.* This tells participants the purpose of the meeting up front, so they know why they are coming and the intended outcome.

2. *Determine who needs to attend the meeting.* Clarify who is a "must have" and who should be invited as backup or extra reinforcement. Be clear when you invite your meeting participants. For example, if an invitee cannot attend the meeting because of a schedule conflict, can a representative attend in his or her place? Will the backup attendee be expected to act with the same level of authority as the original invitee? All of these expectations should be clearly stated in advance of the meeting. If key stakeholders cannot attend, postpone the meeting.

3. *Send out the meeting notice in advance.* For scheduled meetings where advance notice is available, try to provide at least seven days' notice. If prework is required, be specific in stating the requirements. In some instances, detailed instructions might be needed; in other instances, the attendees can attend with little to no advance preparation. Be clear about what you want your participants to know beforehand or what you want them to bring to the meeting.

4. *Pick a neutral location.* This is especially effective if the meeting is called to resolve conflicts or solve complex problems. Select a location where participants are unlikely to be interrupted, if possible. Make sure appropriate seating is arranged and equipment and services are ready and working properly.

Although many of these tips seem obvious, they are often overlooked or ignored, resulting in unnecessary delays and dragging down the meeting's efficiency and effectiveness.

Figure 8-1 is a template for a meeting agenda. It might not look a lot different from what you use today, but there is a difference: It includes a reminder of the team's expected behaviors.

What It Is

The meeting agenda template allows you to organize and plan team meetings so all team members understand what the meeting is about, what is planned during the meeting, and what each participant must do before the meeting.

Why It's Useful

The meeting agenda template keeps meeting participants focused on the issues at hand in a time-efficient manner.

How to Use It

Before the scheduled meeting, distribute the Meeting Agenda, along with any corresponding documents, to all invited meeting participants. Be sure to use the agenda when running the meeting.

<Team or Project Name>

Meeting Agenda

<Logistics: Date, Time, Location, Call-in Numbers>

Attendees:

Facilitator(s):

Overall Meeting Goal:

Expected Behaviors for Team Performance	
Treat others with dignity and respect	Actively seek and receive feedback for improvement
Exchange the needs and impacts of your own work with others	Make timely decisions and solve problems quickly

Figure 8-1 Meeting Agenda Template

Duration	Agenda Topic	Who	Goal

Figure 8-1 Figure 8-1 Meeting Agenda Template (*Continued*)

DURING THE MEETING

Run meetings according to these simple operating rules:

- Start and finish on time.
- Post the meeting's goals and objectives so everyone who attends can see them.
- Capture actions items, owners, and due dates using the RAID process.
- Close with "next steps."

For teams that have rules of engagement in place, it is important to post the rules at each team meeting; a visual reminder helps the team aim for good behavior and efficient operating rules. Some meetings will require new or different participants to address an urgent issue or to make an important decision. For these meetings, there is not enough time to introduce the rules of engagement to the group.

The time allotted to the agenda typically is just long enough to address the issues at hand or make the decision necessary to get the project back on track. In this instance, the best approach is to state one or two ground rules at the outset of the meeting. For example, immediately following a welcome, inform the group of your participation expectations to achieve the meeting goal. You might want to say something like this:

- It is a goal of this session to have equal participation by all members.
- We will go around the group, giving each participant a turn to respond to each question.
- We will need to impose air-time limits on ourselves as participants.
- Does everyone buy into this process?

This four-step process is useful when conducting a meeting:

1. *Present the information.* This includes presenting the purpose of the meeting.
2. *Evaluate the information.* Participants debate the merits of the ideas or facts presented.
3. *Come to a decision/recommendation.* Resolve the problem.
4. *Take action.* The implementation of the decision begins with making assignments and ends with following up on actions decided upon.

Guidance for Facilitators

Meetings don't run on their own. Someone needs to lead the charge and take control. Effective facilitation is critical to ensure successful meeting outcomes. The effective facilitator:

- Functions as a guide
- Holds a neutral position, never taking sides
- Is not the seat of wisdom and knowledge
- Does not express opinions
- Draws out the opinions and ideas of the group
- Is responsible for making everyone feel comfortable
- Makes members feel good about their contributions

- Keeps the group focused on the agenda
- Is able to involve everyone in the meeting by asking probing questions.

When acting as facilitator, it is important to establish your role. Be sure to identify yourself as the meeting facilitator and briefly describe your role to participants. Once you set expectations among the group, it is important to stay in your role; being facilitator means the meeting is never about you, but about the participants who have been invited to the meeting.

The Usual Suspects

Relying on a diverse group of participants means managing a diverse set of personalities. In most meetings, you can anticipate encountering a set of temperaments that will challenge your facilitation skills. The usual suspects include the Disruptor, the Excessive Talker, and the Silent Type.

The Disruptor

The Disruptor is the one who constantly interrupts the meeting by expressing opinions on how to do things differently, or who tells you the meeting is being managed the "wrong" way while he or she has a "better" way to get results. The best way to manage a Disruptor is to get agreement on the process, ground rules, and outcomes early in the meeting.

The ideal way to derail a Disruptor is to get buy-in in advance of the meeting. In other words, give the Disruptor a role to play during the meeting. For example, acknowledge the Disruptor's ability to be persuasive. Enlist his or her help in encouraging the silent participants to open up. Giving Disruptors a role to play realigns their focus on the meeting yet still engages them in an active manner.

If in spite of your preemptive measures the Disruptor continues to dominate the meeting, apply interventions when the disruption is happening. For example, go back to the ground rules or rules of engagement and remind meeting participants of the agreements made at the beginning of the meeting. Be honest. State what is going on, but do not express anger or frustration. In fact, use humor; it often relieves the tension in the group.

The Excessive Talker

When someone dominates a discussion, the other participants in the group hold back their ideas and become bored because of their lack of engagement. The best way to handle an Excessive Talker is to remind the group about air-time limits. Politely interrupt the person with, "We'll see if we have time to get back to that topic, Peter. For now, let's move on." You may also leverage Talkers by enlisting their help to get the silent participants to open up.

The Silent Type

Those who quietly sit in the meeting leave you wondering: "Does Sally have something to say, but is too shy to state it, or is she preoccupied, wanting to be somewhere else?" Silence is hard to read. You can encourage the Silent Types to talk by creating an inclusive atmosphere from the very start of the meeting. When you set a model for equal participation for everyone, it is often hard for someone to not speak up or be actively involved.

You can draw the Silent Types into the meeting by directing questions to them. Make it personal; call them by name. Ask questions related to their area of expertise and interest. This builds confidence in shy participants. You can also encourage involvement by asking them to comment on someone else's statement or by reinforcing their comments (without appearing to be patronizing).

ENDING THE MEETING

You can end a meeting by simply saying, ten minutes before the meeting is over, "Let's wrap it up. We need to be out of here in five minutes."

This gives participants time to organize their thoughts, have a last word, and mentally sum up for themselves what the meeting has meant to them. It also begins the transition to next steps—the actions needed from this point on and how to proceed.

Summarize the proceedings for the group, review the meeting's purpose and ask if it has been achieved, summarize the events, accentuate the positive results, and determine next steps. Deliver your closing comments with energy and power. Be sure to thank the participants. Include a collective thank-you to the group, and also be sure to recognize those who were key contributors to the meeting's success.

ASSESSING THE MEETING

You might think the meeting was a huge success, but others might leave frustrated and less than appreciative about spending their time without reaching a decision that affects them. Without an assessment, there is no way to determine whether the meeting achieved its purpose. In the simplest of terms, the meeting assessment answers three questions:

- What happened?
- What was accomplished?
- What was not accomplished?

Asking your participants to evaluate the meeting can be done quickly. You do not need to ask each participant to spend lots of time filling out a comprehensive report card when the meeting ends. In fact, the shorter, the better.

For teams that have regularly scheduled meetings, it is sometimes easy to fall into following the same standard routine week after week and never take the time to evaluate how the meetings are working. Another way to evaluate meetings is to periodically dedicate ten minutes at the end of a meeting to verbally ask members how the meeting went.

An evaluation does not need to include a formal set of questions, nor does it need to include all participants. However, the act of asking for feedback shows participants that you are constantly looking to create an efficient and effective meeting experience for everyone, and it shows you are willing to make changes based on their comments and observations.

AFTER THE MEETING

Be sure to document and distribute meeting minutes, including action items. This should be done within 24 hours of the meeting, if possible, because prompt meeting follow-up establishes momentum for getting the work done.

The Meeting Minutes template provided in figure 8-2 might be helpful. Like the Meeting Agenda template, it includes a reminder of the team's expected behaviors.

VIRTUAL MEETINGS

Today, the global economy requires meetings with participants who are spread across the country or around the world, raising new challenges for running successful meetings.

Facilitating a meeting face-to-face is still preferred, but today it is not uncommon to run a meeting by phone, videoconferencing, or some other alternative mode of communication. The way we work presents new challenges when we cannot have all participants together in one physical location. Many companies have multiple office locations, with staff working from regional locations across multiple states. Often, companies work with many vendors that are located in other regions of the country. They might also have a number of staff people who work from home.

What It Is

The Meeting Minutes template allows you to organize and document all important activities and/or decisions made during the meeting.

Why It's Useful

The Meeting Minutes template keeps meeting participants focused on the progress made during the meeting and highlights action items required to keep activities progressing between meetings.

How to Use It

Key areas to document include:

- Decisions made
- Open action items
- Closed action items.

Document and distribute all meeting minutes immediately following each meeting. Getting minutes out within 24 hours of the meeting is ideal.

<Team or Project Name>
Meeting Minutes / Results
<Logistics: Date, Time, Location, Call-In Numbers>

Attendees:

Facilitator(s):

Overall Meeting Goal:

Expected Behaviors for Team Performance	
Treat others with dignity and respect	Actively seek and receive feedback for improvement
Exchange the needs and impacts of your own work with others	Make timely decisions and solve problems quickly

Figure 8-2 Meeting Minutes Template

Decisions
•
•
•
•

Open Action Item/Issue	Owner	Due
1.		
2.		
3.		
4.		
5.		

Closed Action Item/Issue	Resolution	Closed
1.		
2.		
3.		
4.		
5.		

Figure 8-2 Meeting Minutes Template (*Continued*)

Running a virtual meeting often forces you to be efficient. You will be more conscientious about running the meeting according to schedule. The need to be efficient, however, is apt to remove some of the intimacy created when everyone is meeting at the same location.

Be sure to take the time to get to know your virtual team members, and use this knowledge to add intimacy to the meeting—just as you would when running a local meeting. It's fine to chitchat with team members who join the call early or first. (This, by the way, highlights the need for you, as the meeting leader, to always arrive on the call early, so you can assume the role of host.)

Consider ways to enhance a level of intimacy among virtual team members. Each time you hear a "ding" when a new caller joins the meeting, does everyone know who just joined? Welcome people as they join, and acknowledge their presence. Ask, "Who just joined us?" each time someone new jumps on. Use visual imagery; comments such as "I can sense you smiling" include participants as if everyone were in the same location.

Do you know what your virtual team members look like? Posting photos is easy with today's technology. Do you know where your virtual team members live? Are they in different time zones? Are you familiar with international holidays, so scheduled meetings don't impact personal time off? What do you know about the other geographic regions represented on the call? Does it snow in the winter? Is it warm in the summer?

When you are the host, take these steps *before* the call:

- Be sure you have set up and confirmed all call details with the service provider.
- Contact all participants in advance and give them the date, time, call-in number with area code, access code, link, any password, and agenda information. Be specific about time zone.
- Begin promptly at the scheduled time. Don't wait for latecomers.
- Depending on the size of the group, take a few minutes to confirm who is on the call and to ensure everyone can see posted visuals and hear participants when they speak.
- Be sure any latecomers introduce themselves as soon as possible during the meeting.
- List who is on the phone so you have a visual view of all participants.
- Watch your tone of voice. It can have a greater impact on effective communications than the words themselves.

- Review the meeting agenda and review basic teleconference etiquette as guidelines for the call. (Use the rules of engagement if in place; the ground rules, as a second option.)

- Be aware of who is participating and who is not. Check in with any quiet participants to find out whether they have an opinion or question.

- Remember to give short breaks during long meetings (five- to ten-minute breaks every 60 to 90 minutes).

- Before ending the meeting, offer the opportunity for final/closing questions or comments; go around the "virtual room" and address each participant by name.

- End the teleconference clearly. Briefly review items discussed, clarify actions to be taken, and instruct participants to hang up.

- End the call promptly.

At a meeting, a little courtesy goes a long way. Some common-sense etiquette tips apply to all participants:

- Be on time.

- Plan to talk from a quiet location; avoid background noise.

- Use the "mute" button on your phone when you are not speaking, but remember to un-mute when you want to talk. Know where the button is on your phone. Nothing is worse than that few extra seconds of dead silence as you frantically search to release the right button when under duress.

- Avoid using cellular and cordless phones. They can create annoying static and sometimes lose reception.

- Always identify yourself when you speak.

- Address people by name when you speak to them. Remember, there are no visual cues over the phone. It can be very difficult to determine who is being addressed.

- Avoid putting your phone on hold during the teleconference, especially if you're calling from a phone that plays music.

- Turn off the phone's call waiting feature before you join the conference call.
- Let people know that you are leaving the call. Don't just drop off.
- If you are participating from a cubicle, use the handset and not the speaker feature of your phone.
- If you are calling from a room with a door, close it for extended calls.

It's a Virtual World

With team members dispersed across the globe, how do you keep everyone involved? It is critically important that all team members participate in the rules of engagement exercise. Understand that virtual team members might have different needs and concerns than their co-located team members. It is important to allow everyone the opportunity to voice their needs and issues.

Try to consider the needs of your virtual team members because sometimes it is hard for us to fully appreciate the unique requirements of our distant colleagues. For example, when you conduct a virtual team meeting, how long does your meeting last? Do meetings go on for longer than an hour? What do your virtual team members do when they need to use the restroom? Do they place the phone on "mute," quickly disappear, and hope they won't be called on during their absence? Why not schedule a formal break during a virtual meeting, allowing all members the equal opportunity to move about, stretch their legs, or conduct activities we all take for granted when we can easily see one another in the room?

How many times have you been on a conference call, only to lose the connection midway through the meeting? Does your team have a Plan B in place, so everyone knows who reinstates the call and how it will happen? Or how about when someone places the call on hold, only to interrupt the entire meeting when everyone on the connection must listen to the Muzak over the open line?

Creating a common experience among virtual team members and co-located members is difficult but important. Making everyone on the team feel visible, even when not seen, creates a level of equality and produces engagement among team members.

I recently visited a client location where the entire organization had adopted a new policy regarding virtual teams. Regardless of where team members are located, all participants are required to call in to meetings. It doesn't matter if you are calling from across the country or across the corridor. All members act as virtual team members.

The reason for this shift is to create a culture that levels the playing field for all team members. It forces those who previously had the luxury of sitting in the same conference room around one table to stand in their virtual team members' shoes. The company has created a number of operating policies to support the "it's a virtual world" culture. While this may seem extreme to some, it appears to be working for this organization.

Mandating a totally virtual world might not be feasible for all, but it does have some benefits. Some studies suggest that team members located across different cities and countries often outperform teams with small levels of dispersion. For example, team members who are located in the same building but work on different floors don't consider themselves dispersed and might under-appreciate or under-plan virtual relationships. Team members who work at great physical distances are often more aware of the challenges associated with their separation and make greater efforts to communicate and collaborate.

This is not to say that conducting virtual meetings is easy. There are a multitude of possible scenarios that create interruptions for virtual team meetings. Rules of engagement might not eliminate all possible situations, but they can certainly reduce the distractions that will occur, taking everyone off task and reducing team productivity and effectiveness. With more than two-thirds of business professionals engaging in virtual work, virtual meetings are a standard feature for the business landscape for most.

Here are four lessons I have learned while conducting business from the road:

1. *Be prepared.* Make sure you (and those you are conducting business with) have what is needed, when you need it. Nothing is worse than launching into a business discussion without having the necessary materials or information available. Distribute all materials in advance of the meeting. No one wants to hear, "Sorry you can't see this, but...."

2. *Be friendly.* Establishing rapport from a distance can be difficult, but it can be done if meeting participants make an effort to engage with their virtual colleagues. Remember to greet all participants by name as soon as they join the call; phantom callers never get the recognition they deserve. Take time for small talk as you are waiting for remaining meeting participants to join the call. Engage in casual conversation just as you would if they were sitting next to you. It's amazing how much you will learn about the other person during brief chitchat.

Some possible topics are listed below:

- What's your favorite music?
- What's your favorite TV show?
- What was the last movie you saw?
- Where is your favorite vacation destination?
- What's your "dream car"?
- Do you have a hobby?
- Do you drink coffee or tea?
- What's your favorite breakfast food?
- What's your current weather?
- What do you see around you?

- Do you volunteer?
- Are you a "morning person"?
- What was your favorite childhood pet? What was its name?
- Name a famous person you have a connection with and explain the connection.

3. *Be visible.* Do you know what your virtual teammates look like? Launch a photo shoot. Have everyone take a quick head shot using a cell phone and exchange pictures. The bond between teammates will strengthen when there is a face with a name.

4. *Be equipped.* If using technology to support the call, know how to use it. Be familiar with all systems in advance of initiating the meeting, and make sure you know what to do or who to contact should the equipment fail. At the very least, be sure all participants know what to do in the event the meeting is prematurely disconnected—always have a plan B in place.

Virtual Leadership

The 21st century project manager needs to inspire, challenge, motivate, and innovate. Successful project managers must learn how to leverage the diversity of team members to meet growing project challenges. As previously noted, there are benefits to be gained from different perspectives, opinions, and points of view. Teams that are open to different perspectives and value healthy differences are positioned to win in business today.

Globalization introduces new challenges to project team dynamics. If lack of face time with individual team members is difficult, imagine having to lead a team with members in different cities, perhaps even different countries, who have never met in person. How do you turn a geographically dispersed team into a cohesive team?

Globalization enables business partners to easily connect from virtually anywhere in the world. The ease of connectability, however, also increases cultural diversity on teams, creating new and unexpected challenges among team members. Diversity is not just about race, religion, or social practices. It entails all aspects of what makes people different, which can be found in any group of people, even if initially the group does not appear very diverse at all. For team leaders who are responsible for leading global teams but have limited international exposure, diversity creates challenges in establishing sound team dynamics.

As children, with limited experiences, our view of the world is fairly fluid. What is accepted as fact one day will be discarded another day in favor of something new. As we get older, however, our combined experiences tend to result in attitudes that become more ingrained. Often, only a major event will dramatically change our perception of the world in which we live or the world we view from afar.

Our perception is our reality; our day-to-day experiences, our religious beliefs, and our social interactions often define our view of the world. Therefore, our limited view often makes it difficult for us to see something from someone else's perspective or reality.

One of the ironies of diversity is that we all tend to assume that people who are different from us understand how and why we think and behave the way we do. We take for granted the way we are, and we expect others to synergize with us and to see things from our viewpoint.

When establishing global teams that comprise diverse members, there are four key areas to consider:

1. *Communication and language.* Communication, both verbal and nonverbal, distinguishes one group from another. Languages can be differentiated through dialect, slang, or jargon. Communication can occur in the absence of words, through body language, hand gestures, or facial expressions.

2. *Time.* Different cultures view time and practice time management quite differently. Generally, Germans are precise about time, while Latins are casual. In some cultures, time is managed by minutes and

hours, while in others it is measured in days. Some cultures manage time by seniority or age, while others measure by sunrise or sunset. Some industries manage time through shifts, while others maintain strict 9-to-5 schedules.

3. *Religion.* Religious practices sometimes become apparent in business practices. Religious holidays, for example, must be considered when establishing business meeting schedules. Religious tolerance is critically important among team members; unconditional acceptance of all members, regardless of religious affiliation, is a must to ensure team harmony and mutual respect.

4. *Social practices.* People from different cultures have different ways of expressing themselves and interacting with others. For example, in the United States, a firm, short handshake indicates self-confidence. In most parts of Africa, however, a limp handshake is the correct way to do it.

Under ideal circumstances, all team leaders who are responsible for managing global teams should be familiar with the lifestyle and practices of their global team members. Unfortunately, time is of the essence; most project teams must hit the ground running upon project assignment. Little to no time is available to investigate new countries, new cultures, or new social practices to adequately prepare project managers responsible for managing global teams. Unless a team leader has previous experience with a foreign country or different region, much of his or her appreciation for cultural differences will occur when conflicts arise.

The good news is that many project teams indicate that the multicultural makeup of a global group is not a major success factor or a major hindrance to project success. Perhaps this is because we, as team members, expect differences when entering a team of visibly diverse team members. In fact, today's global corporations embrace the strategic importance of multicultural work groups. By expanding across the globe, companies and teams are able to access deeper talent pools, produce more innovative opportunities, and reduce costs through economies of scale.

When dealing with a culturally diverse team and time is of the essence, there are a few techniques a team leader can use to introduce team members to cultural diversity and to enhance appreciation of team differences. For example, when kicking off a new global team, why not introduce a fun yet informative way for team members to appreciate one another? Use a diversity quiz to break the ice among team members and allow team members to share information about their respective lives. The process enables discovery of real practical, local diversity issues; educates all team members to the extent of diverse membership; and dispels some of the preconceived notions of cultural practices or social beliefs.

Establish a set of questions to pose to team members. The quiz can occur all at once as a way to kick off the team, or you can kick off each team meeting with a new question. The approach itself is not important; sharing information and increasing members' awareness of cultural differences is what counts.

The questions should be simple—focused on the everyday things we all take for granted, except when it comes to other people (which is precisely the reason for asking them). When you are managing geographically dispersed teams, the obvious questions are related to geographical/cultural facts. Here are some topics to consider:

- National holidays
- Capital cities
- Language
- Money/currency
- Religious practices
- National sports/hobbies/pastimes
- Music/dance
- Weather/climate/seasons

- National flag/national anthem
- Local animals/birds/plants.

When selecting questions, consider the types of diversity you might have on your team. For example, diversity is not limited to geographical distance. Consider age or generational factors, members who have children or who are childless, lifestyle preferences, etc.

As the team congeals and the members feel more comfortable with each other, ask the team members to suggest questions. Developing the questions is not the most important aspect of the process; it's the sharing of information that holds the greatest potential for mutual understanding, respect, and acceptance—all leading to high-performing teamwork.

THE GENERATION GAP

We can't ignore the new generation and how it affects our business teams. The Next Gen, also known as Gen Y, represents the young people entering the workforce over the past few years. They have a new set of expectations and a high level of confidence when expressing their needs. Adding the Next Gen to our teams is both necessary and challenging. Gen Y members have a different world view and different approaches to getting work done; other team members must adapt to their addition to the team.

Stereotypes about the youngest generation entering the workforce are less than flattering. Gen Y has been labeled self-absorbed, entitled, and individually focused. The younger generation is not without its challenges, but what group isn't? The key is to leverage the differences the Gen Y'ers bring to the team to enhance output and collaboration.

Consider the following Gen Y characteristics when working with groups with a large Gen Y membership:

1. *High energy and expectations.* Younger members inject high levels of energy. Their eagerness and excitement are contagious; they often lift others in spirit and morale. They aim to work faster and better than other workers. They want small goals with tight deadlines so they can build up ownership of tasks.

2. *Tech-savvy.* Gen Y has a natural understanding and confidence with technology that many of us cannot beat, including the well-trained technologists on our team. They love technology and are used to operating in an interconnected world through use of the Internet and cell phones. Often referred to as "digital natives," they have grown up surrounded by technology, unlike older workers, referred to as "digital immigrants." They know time-saving tech shortcuts capable of shaving significant time off getting things done and rely on collaborative tools to communicate. Leverage their expertise to enhance team collaboration and communication.

3. *Flexible.* The younger generation is not stuck in the 9-to-5 schedule; they tend to live a 24/7 schedule. They have all the latest technology and gadgets, making it easy for them to stay connected and available to meet team needs all the time. Younger workers can be just as productive during informal sessions as during formal business meetings. They adapt to their environment well and easily adapt to multiple communication styles. They are used to getting information from many different information sources and can easily filter what they have discovered. They value freedom of choice and perform best when faced with options.

4. *More accepting.* The younger generations is accustomed to a global environment. They have been raised in culturally diverse environments and have little difficulty accepting individual differences when working with others. They are capable of multitasking and are less "hung up" on standardized operating rules. They desire freedom with respect to how to best get the work done. They are more accepting of multiple learning styles and are more open to new ideas and different strategies for getting the job done.

BRIDGING THE FUNCTIONAL DIVIDE

Team members from functional organizations who report to their functional managers during the project have a conflict of interest, and the supervisor's needs often win over the project's needs. Virtual teams can exacerbate the issue because the functional manager of a virtual team member has direct face time with his or her staff, sustaining a tight alignment with the functional department versus the virtual relationship with the project and the project team leader.

Technology can successfully link virtual team members, yet not without additional commitment of resources and investment of time. Online video conferencing and computer desktop sharing services/software, such as Skype, WebEx, and Conference + Netmeeting tools, can create intimacy among virtual team members—but only when everyone knows how to use the technology.

Content Management Systems (CMS) are also effective in managing project documentation. A CMS, project Wiki, and Document Management System are all different versions of technology that do the same thing: They provide a storage area for project documentation during the life of the project. They are particularly important to virtual teams when timely review and edits to project documentation are critical to the success of the project, but they are challenging to manage with virtual team members.

All team members must have a firm understanding of tool use, security settings, and user functionality to make these systems work effectively. Be sure all virtual team members are adequately informed on the tool selected and have support services when they need help. Technology policies can restrict what you see, what you can use, and how to access information.

Be sure to vet corporate policies, particularly for the external parties, vendors, or consultants that might be on your team. Likewise, technologies can be different and differently accepted across divisions working together on the same project. Be sure to investigate all potential road-blocks before you launch a virtual team.

All project team leaders must consider the operational challenges associated with virtual team management and understand the challenges associated with cultural differences to successfully guide the team toward efficient and effective project results.

Four Last Words

Be prepared for different.

No matter how much you prepare, something on your team might (and probably will) go differently from the way you planned it. How you handle the unexpected will make the difference between success and failure. Team failures occur when you, as the team leader, call attention to the issue or let it ruin the rest of the meeting or impact long-term working relationships. Team members look to you for guidance, advice, and expertise. How you react or respond to the unexpected sets the tone for the entire team and often defines your success as a leader. When team meetings fail to occur as smoothly as you planned, never lose your cool. Take a few minutes to get everyone back on track, and do so calmly and with authority.

Organizations that invest in healthy team dynamics and hold team members accountable for meeting expectations say it makes a difference. Teams that identify their strengths and weaknesses early and work together to flag and fix team behaviors enhance their performance and improve their results—a winning combination for success.

The tools and templates in this book and a variety of process tips and techniques to support healthy teams are available to download at www.yourprojectoffice.com. To access these resources, click on "Client Login" and enter username "Reader" and password "Team1." All the tools are formatted in MS Word or Excel, so no special software is required. If you have trouble accessing the site or its resources, please contact support@yourprojectoffice.com.

Index

Delivering Project Excellence with the Statement of Work, Second Edition
Michael G. Martin, PMP

This second edition builds on the foundation of the first edition with a comprehensive yet succinct description of how to develop and apply the statement of work (SOW) to manage projects effectively. With updates throughout and an entirely new chapter on the use and application of the statement of objectives, this book continues to serve as a practical guide for project managers and team members. The new edition includes coverage of project management issues related to the federal government such as updated FAR guidance on drafting a quality SOW and a discussion of legal considerations related to the SOW. New examples of SOWs from a variety of types of projects and business environments add to the second edition's usefulness.

ISBN 978-1-56726-257-5 ■ Product Code B575 ■ 300 pages

The 77 Deadly Sins of Project Management
Management Concepts

Projects can be negatively impacted by common "sins" that hinder, stall, or throw the project off track. *The 77 Deadly Sins of Project Management* helps you better understand how to execute projects by providing individual anecdotes and case studies of the project management sins described by experts in the field.

ISBN 978-1-56726-246-9 ■ Product Code B777 ■ 357 pages

Managing Complex Projects: A New Model
Kathleen B. Hass, PMP

For organizations to thrive, indeed to survive, in today's global economy, we must find ways to dramatically improve the performance of large-scale projects. *Managing Complex Projects: A New Model* offers an innovative way of looking at projects and treating them as complex adaptive systems. Applying the principles of complexity thinking will enable project managers and leadership teams to manage large-scale initiatives successfully. ***Winner of the 2009 Project Management Institute David I. Cleland Project Management Literature Award.***

ISBN 978-1-56726-233-9 ■ Product Code B339 ■ 298 pages

Essential People Skills for Project Managers
Ginger Levin, PMP, DPA, and Steven Flannes, PhD

Essential People Skills for Project Managers brings the key concepts of interpersonal skills into sharp focus, offering specific, practical skills that you can grasp quickly, apply immediately, and use to resolve difficult people issues. Derived from the widely popular original book, *People Skills for Project Managers*, this new version provides condensed content and a practical focus.

ISBN 978-1-56726-168-4 ■ Product Code B68X ■ 181 pages